# Minimum
# Wages

# Minimum Wages
## Measures and Industry Effects

John M. Peterson

American Enterprise Institute for Public Policy Research
Washington and London

John M. Peterson is a professor of economics at Ohio University, Athens, Ohio.

Distributed to the Trade by National Book Network, 15200 NBN Way, Blue Ridge Summit, PA 17214. To order call toll free 1-800-462-6420 or 1-717-794-3800. For all other inquiries please contact the AEI Press, 1150 Seventeenth Street, N.W., Washington, D.C. 20036 or call 1-800-862-5801.

Library of Congress Cataloging in Publication Data

Peterson, John M., 1922–
  Minimum wages.

    (AEI studies ; 331)
    1.  Wages—Minimum wage—United States.  I. Title.
II. Series.
HD4918.P48          331.2′3          81-8001
                                     AACR2
ISBN 0-8447-3455-1
ISBN 0-8447-3453-5 (pbk.)

AEI Studies 331

*Printed in the United States of America*

# Contents

LIST OF TABLES

LIST OF FIGURES

might be expected to be large enough to be demonstrated. More recently economists have used time series regression analysis to identify effects on low-wage worker groups. Usually attention is focused on youth, blacks, and females.[1]

So far the research efforts have succeeded in demonstrating convincingly that the direction of employment effects predicted by theory is empirically supported. Some uncertainty remains, however, about the size of the disemployment effects. This seems to arise from differences in the statistical methods used—that is, in the specification of variables in multiple-regression equations. The size of elasticity estimates derived from these regressions also varies. Legislators may want more precision and agreement in the estimates by experts in order to have confidence in their results.[2] Since the size of the elasticity estimate is usually below unity, this also lends support to the claims of proponents that the wage benefits to workers generally exceed the disemployment losses to a few.

Economists, of course, have not let the public policy argument end at this point. A minimum wage remains an incomplete social reform tool without an accompanying method of helping the disemployed. A minimum may also be an inefficient method of assisting low-income families because of a lack of close correspondence between low wage rates and low annual family incomes. Edward M. Gramlich has presented evidence that most youths receiving below-minimum wage rates are in families with above-average incomes. Many youths also get above-minimum wages. Gramlich has also provided a theoretical basis for calculating a welfare break-even elasticity level that is much lower than unity. Considering job turnover, length of unemployment, and the transfer payments to the unemployed, he has estimated a welfare break-even elasticity criterion for youth as low as —0.34.[3]

[1] A summary of early studies was presented by John M. Peterson and Charles T. Stewart, Jr., *Employment Effects of Minimum Wage Rates* (Washington, D.C.: American Enterprise Institute, 1969). Some later studies were cited by Hyman Kaitz in U.S. Department of Labor, Bureau of Labor Statistics, *Youth Unemployment and Minimum Wages*, bulletin 1657 (1970), chap. 2. Still later studies were cited by Finis Welch, *Minimum Wages: Issues and Evidence* (Washington, D.C.: American Enterprise Institute, 1978).

[2] Robert S. Goldfarb, "The Policy Content of Quantitative Minimum Wage Research," in *Proceedings of the Twenty-seventh Annual Meetings* (Madison, Wis.: Industrial and Labor Relations Research Association, 1974), pp. 261–68.

[3] Gramlich cites elasticity estimates between —0.05 and —0.25. His own estimate for youth was —0.09, the lower-bound break-even elasticity criterion for this group being —0.34. See Edward M. Gramlich, "Impact of Minimum Wages on Other Wages, Employment, and Family Incomes," *Brookings Papers on Economic Activity*, no. 2 (1976), pp. 409–51.

Improved estimates of elasticity, nevertheless, are needed. In this regard, Gramlich may have performed an even greater service in questioning whether elasticity is being underestimated. For the estimates of employment changes in the numerator of the elasticity ratio, he finds that an underestimate tends to result from failing to distinguish full-time employment from part-time employment. Youth seems to have experienced less full-time employment under the minimums.[4] This recalls the correctness of the emphasis in earlier minimum-wage studies of the need to measure the quantity of labor employed in man-hours rather than just in numbers of workers. Not capturing the full employment effect underestimates the elasticity ratio. For the estimates of the wage changes in the denominator of the elasticity ratio, Gramlich also argues that it is incorrect to use the log form for coverage weights in the minimum-wage measure. An overestimate of the wage increase imposed by the minimum wage also would underestimate the elasticity.

This questioning of the measure of the increase imposed by the minimum wage is important, because most recent studies have used the same formula for measuring the minimum wage as a variable in regressions. The formula was developed by the Bureau of Labor Statistics (BLS) for taking account of two applicable minimum-wage levels with different coverage ratios among industries. The possible errors in this conventional measure as well as the neglect of man-hour data provided the stimulus for this study.

**Overview of This Study.** This study proposes to develop a new measure of the minimum-wage variable and to apply it to industry data where man-hour measures are available. Chapter 2 begins with a description and criticism of the present measures used in time series regression studies. Usually the minimum-wage rate is deflated by dividing by the average wage. This relative minimum fails to reflect the disproportionate increase in wage costs imposed by raises in the minimum, and it cannot show the level below which a minimum is ineffective. The method first developed by the BLS of combining minimum-wage rates with coverage ratios by industry also uses a weighting procedure that feeds some of the effects back into the measure of what is supposed to be their cause. This has become the conventional measure most widely used.

Chapter 3 then proposes a new minimum-wage measure, called the relative minimum-wage impact. It uses a concept long inherent in

---

[4] For youth in full-time employment, Gramlich estimates an elasticity of —0.50 and a lower-bound break-even elasticity criterion of —0.20.

Labor Department estimates of the payroll increase required by a minimum wage before any adjustments occur. A simple linear model is used to define a formula for this measure. Then two forms of the measure are developed: (1) an overall form directly using the Labor Department's periodic estimates of payroll increases required because of the minimums and (2) an industry-weighted form using a 1970 wage-structure survey of the Labor Department. The industry-weighted form of the new minimum-wage measure and an adjusted form of the conventional minimum-wage measure are then selected for testing on industry data.

Chapter 4 presents regression estimates of the wage, employment, and man-hour effects of minimum wages using the two alternative minimum-wage measures. The approach is intended to demonstrate that a breakdown of aggregate data is needed to show the heavier burden of effects on the lower-wage industries. While the economywide effects for all private nonfarm industry are almost imperceptible, the new minimum-wage measure succeeds in providing significant estimates of a positive influence on average wages and a negative influence on man-hours. Extending the analysis to a breakdown of data for the eight major industry divisions, the new minimum-wage measure helps identify the three divisions that are substantially affected by the minimum: retail trade, finance, and services. Significant positive effects on average wages are found in the regressions for retail trade and finance but not for services. Significant negative effects on employment and man-hours are found only for retail trade, but this lowest-wage division accounts for about one-third of the estimated man-hour losses for all private nonfarm industries.

Chapter 5 attempts a breakdown of data in a high-wage division, manufacturing, in order to show the effects on low-wage industries within that division. Again the new measure provides an identification of six low-wage industries that could be expected to be affected by the minimums. As in previous studies, a significant positive effect is found on average wages, and significant negative effects are found on both employment and man-hours in most of these low-wage industries. Another study is cited showing that although disemployment effects are not necessarily heavier in the South within these low-wage industries, the effects on low-wage industries are apparent in both North and South. Long-term effects on the South, however, are not revealed by the time series regression method.

In all these empirical results, the new minimum-wage measure usually provides more significant estimates of the minimum-wage effects. Often the man-hour effects are more substantial than the employment effects. And in the lowest-wage industries, the elasticity estimates using the new minimum-wage measure are much larger than with the conventional minimum-wage measure.

One implication of these findings for researchers is that in measuring minimum-wage effects on worker groups, it is important to estimate the group average wage and the share of workers below the minimum. Another implication for legislators is the need for caution in legislating step rises because of the disproportionate rise in cost impacts. It is false to expect uniform estimates of elasticity from experts when the size of disemployment effects varies with the severity of minimum-wage impacts and with different industry demands.

# 2

# The Commonly Used Minimum-Wage Measures

The history of periodic raises in federal minimum-wage rates facilitates the use of time series regressions to isolate their effects. Since the passage of the Fair Labor Standards Act in 1938 there have been six amendments, each raising the level of the minimum-wage rates initially and sometimes phasing in further step increases in subsequent years. Extensions in the percentage of all jobs covered by the law also have occurred in 1961, 1967, and 1974. With each of these extensions a second level of minimum-wage rates has been used to bring the newly covered jobs toward the basic minimum in stages. These are shown in figure 1.

Because the inflation during World War II quickly made the initial minimums of 1938 and 1939 ineffective and because more complete continuous data series began in the postwar period, most regression studies are limited to the postwar years. Yet, under the six amendments passed during the thirty-three years from 1947 through 1979, there were sixteen years with rate increases—nine with a single rate raised and seven with two levels of rates raised.

A problem with studying the effects of these rate increases, however, has been that they involved varying degrees of cost pressure or effectiveness. At the same time other strong economic forces have been raising general wage levels independently. If the trend of average hourly earnings in all private nonfarm industries is plotted alongside the step increases of the minimum, it can be seen that the minimums have been increased at about the same pace as general wages.

## Deflated Minimum-Wage Measures

The approach used initially in time series regressions was to deflate the minimum. This makes the measure of the minimum-wage variable a pure ratio: the minimum-wage rate divided by an average wage. The data used for the average wage are the average hourly earnings of all

## FIGURE 1

### Minimum-Wage Rates and Average Hourly Earnings, 1947–1981

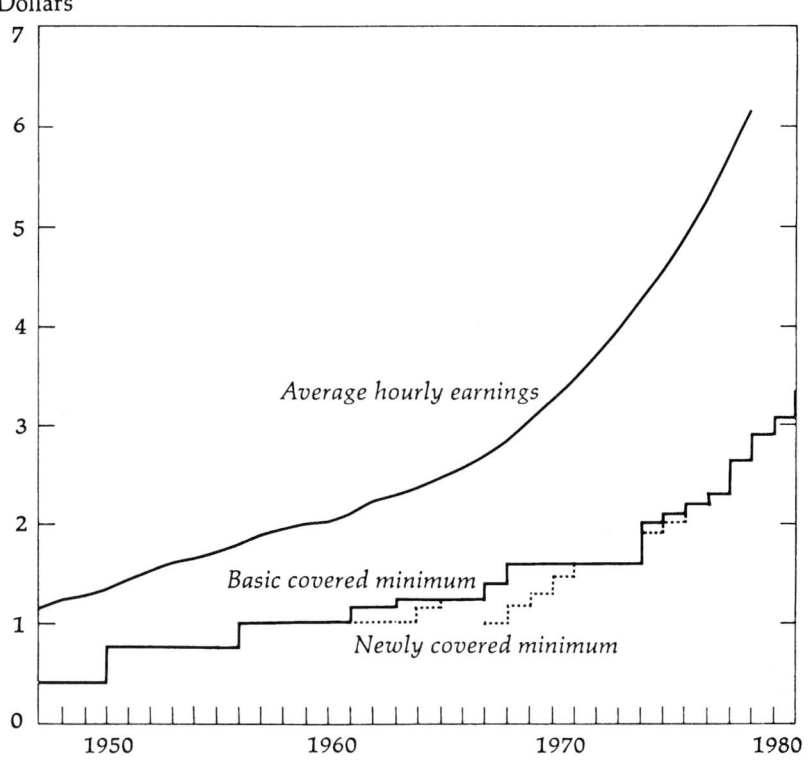

NOTE: Average hourly earnings are for private nonfarm industries. Newly covered groups initially were consolidated with basic covered groups after 1966.
SOURCE: Appendix tables 13 and 14.

private nonfarm industries or, alternatively, the average hourly earnings of manufacturing alone. Since a single basic minimum-wage rate is usually used in this approach, the additional minimum-wage rates used to phase in newly covered groups are ignored. The measure may be referred to as the relative basic minimum wage, or $MB/W$.

The historical pattern of this relative basic minimum has had a saw-toothed fluctuation around a constant level over time. Each increase in the basic minimum caused the ratio to jump up, and the upward trend of average wages gradually lowered it again. The ratio varied between extremes of 0.31 and 0.55, as shown in figure 2.

An alternative way to deflate the basic minimum-wage rate that is sometimes used is to divide the minimum by a price index. This

## FIGURE 2
### Relative Basic Minimum Wage, 1947–1979

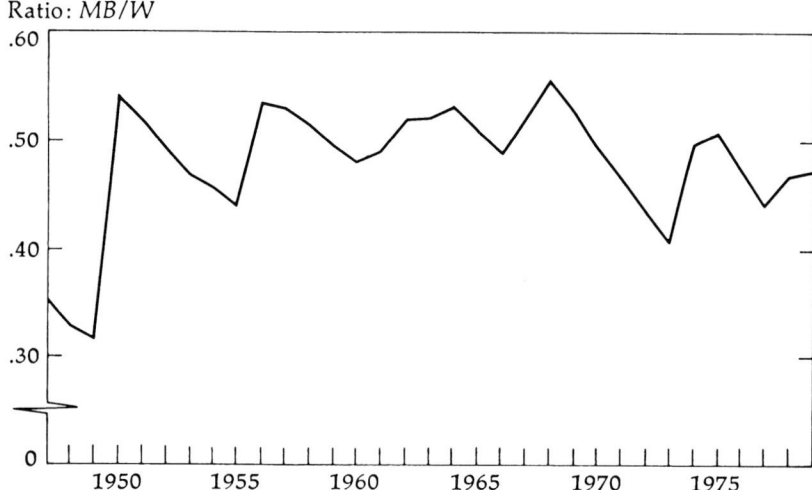

Ratio: $MB/W$

Source: See appendix table 14.

measure may be called the real basic minimum wage, or $MB/P$. The historical pattern of this measure also was saw-toothed, but it has a rising long-term trend, as shown in figure 3. The trend is due to productivity increases that bring a general progress in wage levels relative to price levels throughout the economy. This trend in the minimum-wage measure is a disadvantage statistically for researchers trying to isolate the effect of a minimum from other variables with rising trends.

### The Conventional Measure

The simple deflation approach ignores not only the additional rates for newly covered jobs but also the increase in coverage they involve. Federal legislation has exempted very small firms, some industry classifications, and some occupations from the minimum-wage requirements. This has created for each industry a different coverage ratio, or $E_c/E = C$. The Labor Department has published these ratios for each major industry division. For all private nonfarm employment, the average ratio was about 61 percent in 1950, jumped to 69 percent in 1961, reached 83 percent in 1967, and was 86 percent in 1978, as shown in figure 4.

It is important to take account of this coverage if the minimum is to be deflated by an average wage for all workers. It should be

8

## FIGURE 3
### REAL BASIC MINIMUM WAGE, 1947–1979

Dollars (in 1972 prices)

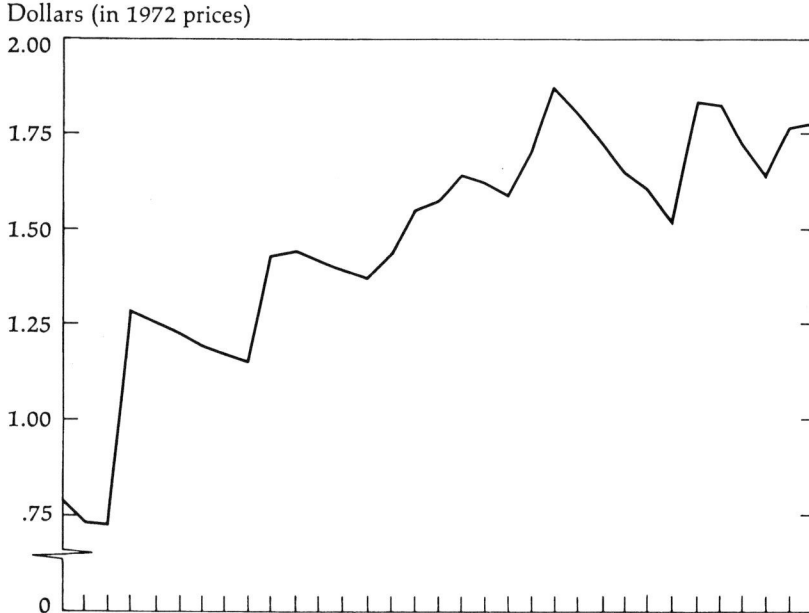

SOURCE: See appendix table 14.

noted that multiplying the minimum-wage rate by a rising coverage ratio not only reduces the size of the relative minimum-wage measure but also gives it a rising trend.

The fact that newly covered worker groups were phased in with lower minimum-wage rates and step increases in different years further complicates the minimum-wage measure. A weighted average minimum applicable to all workers must be used to deflate by an overall average wage. Accordingly, the BLS developed a formula for an overall minimum-wage measure annually or quarterly.[1] In each major industry division, separate ratios are computed for (1) the basic minimum-wage rate times its coverage ratio divided by the industry average wage and (2) the minimum-wage rate for newly covered workers times its coverage ratio divided by the industry average wage. These two ratios are summed for each industry. Then, the combined

[1] Initially presented in U.S. Department of Labor, Bureau of Labor Statistics, *Youth Unemployment and Minimum Wages*, bulletin 1657 (1970), p. 12.

## FIGURE 4
### Percentage of Workers Covered by Minimum Wages, 1950–1978

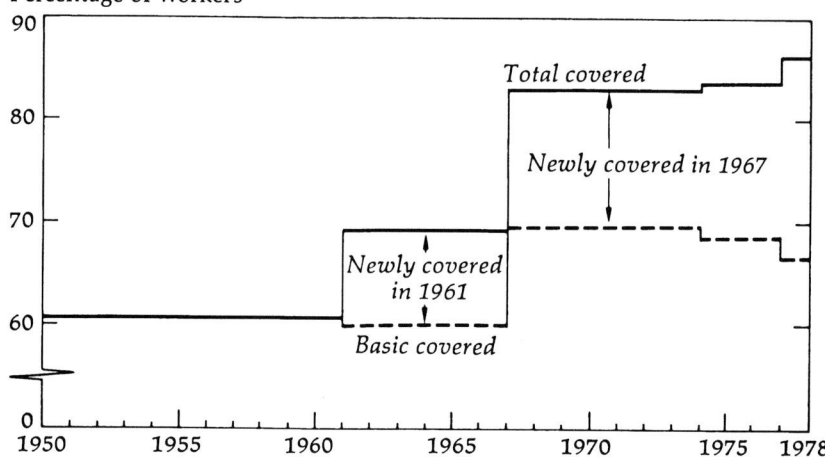

Source: See appendix table 15.

ratio is weighted by the employment share of that industry, and the weighted ratios are summed for all industries, as follows:

$$\Sigma \, (E_i/E) \, [(CB_i \times MB/W_i) + (CN_i \times MN/W_i)]$$

This measure may be referred to as a coverage-weighted relative minimum wage, or $MC/W$.

The historical pattern of this measure showed saw-toothed fluctuations around a slightly rising trend, as shown in figure 5. The rising trend undoubtedly results from the influence of increased coverage. The peaks were at about the same levels in 1950 and 1961–1963, but the peaks were substantially higher in 1968 and in 1978. The advantage of combining dual rates and coverage in a single measure was widely recognized; so most subsequent regression studies have used this minimum-wage measure.

For studying the effects of the minimum wage on youth employment, a different distribution of employment among industries may be relevant.[2] Youth is employed more heavily in service and retail trade

---

[2] Alan A. Fisher, however, presents evidence that minimums account for only a small part of youth unemployment, which was already large in the late 1940s and increased in the 1950s and 1960s for reasons independent of the minimum. See Alan A. Fisher, "The Problem of Teenage Unemployment" (Ph.D. diss., University of California–Berkeley, 1973), prepared for Manpower Administration, September 1973 (processed, National Technical Information Service no. PB 223914).

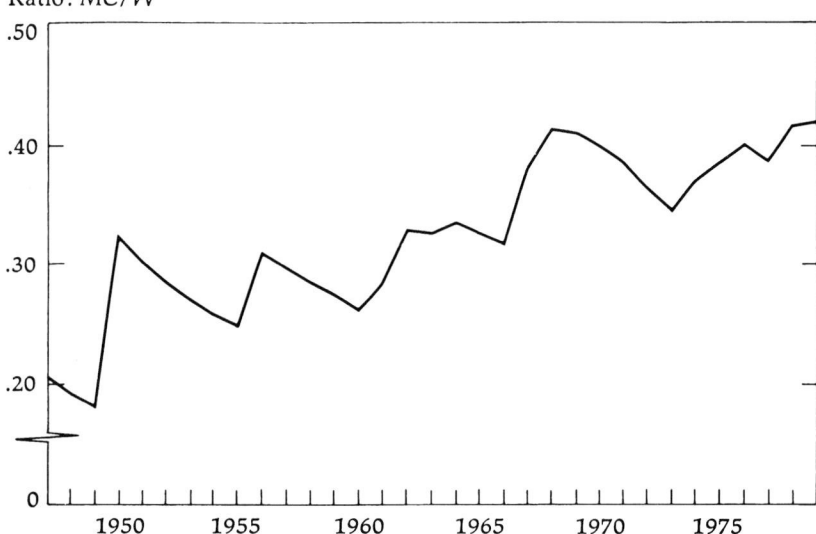

FIGURE 5

COVERAGE-WEIGHTED RELATIVE MINIMUM WAGE, 1947–1979

Ratio: *MC/W*

SOURCE: See appendix table 21.

industries, where coverage increased after 1961. Thus, an alternative version of the BLS minimum-wage measure uses youth employment shares by industry as weights in the formula above. This measure had an even more steeply rising trend, and the data for it have been available for fewer years.

## Modified Measures

**Modifications for the Uncovered Sector.** The lack of complete coverage in the minimum-wage legislation leads to consideration in theory of how the minimums affect the uncovered sector of an industry. Assuming that both sectors have the same pre-minimum-wage equilibrium wage for below-minimum-wage workers, the minimum will raise the wage in the covered sector and lower the wage in the uncovered sector. This is because the disemployed workers from the covered sector increase the supply to the uncovered sector where they can be employed only at a lower wage. An identification problem arises because wage data are available only for a total industry, which averages effects on covered and uncovered sectors. This also obscures and reduces the severity of observed employment effects.

11

Most efforts to account for coverage, however, have been directed at adjusting the coverage ratio in the minimum-wage measure itself.

Finis Welch has modeled this to indicate a need for intensifying the importance of the coverage ratio by expressing it as the fraction $C/(1 - C)$.[3] The denominator shows that the declining fraction of jobs available in the uncovered sector makes it increasingly difficult for that sector to absorb disemployed workers from the increasing fraction of covered employments. This fraction would increase faster than the $C$ ratio alone as a weight in the relative minimum-wage measure.

Welch also developed his model to have implications for the wage in the uncovered sector depending upon two assumptions of supply elasticity. If supply is infinitely elastic, then his minimum-wage measure formula is $1 + C\widetilde{w}$ (where the increase imposed by the minimum wage is $\widetilde{w}$), and only the coverage ratio for the covered sector is relevant. If supply elasticity is unity, however, his minimum-wage measure formula is $1 + [C\widetilde{w}^2/([1 - C] + \widetilde{w})]$.

Gramlich modified Welch's theoretical model to allow for unemployment, which he attaches solely to the covered sector. Using search theory, one finds that unemployment is affected by the turnover rate and the average length of spells of unemployment. Then supply elasticity and withdrawals from the labor force are affected by the replacement-income ratio due to transfer payments.[4] But Gramlich's model also uses the coverage factor $(1 - C)$ for the uncovered sector; and he warns that coverage terms should not be in log form. Still, Gramlich did not use his theoretical modeling in his empirical regression equations. He merely used a dummy variable for coverage and separated it from his minimum-wage measure, the real basic minimum.

**Modifications for Wage Distribution.** Any relative minimum-wage measure has the advantage of requiring data only on a known minimum and an observed average wage. Actually, in each firm and industry there will be a distribution of workers receiving a range of different wage rates. Only the few workers at the low-wage end of the distribution are required by legislation to have their rates raised to the minimum. How, then, is theory modeled to derive implicit predictions of effects only from a ratio of minimum to average wage?

The simplifying assumption implied by use of a relative

---

[3] Finis Welch, "Minimum Wage Legislation in the United States," *Economic Inquiry*, vol. 12, no. 3 (September 1974), pp. 285–318.
[4] Fisher, "Problem of Teenage Unemployment," also points to family income and composition as supply-side variables needed in a regression equation.

minimum-wage measure is that there are two classes of workers. Most workers are high-skill, with above-minimum wage rates. Low-skill workers have below-minimum wage rates, which are some constant proportion of the all-worker average wage. Thus, a minimum wage imposes a wage increase only for these low-skill workers, and the change in the ratio of minimum to average wage is presumed to provide an index of the increased cost of hiring low-skill workers. The amount of labor cost increase, or increase in the average wage, is left unspecified.

Where employment data are available for some identifiable group of presumably low-skill workers, such as youth, the increase in the relative minimum is predicted to affect their employment negatively. A regression estimate of the percentage decrease in employment divided by the percentage increase in the relative minimum is presumed to measure the elasticity of demand for these workers.

One weakness of this approach is the lack of identity between low-skill workers generally and a particular demographic group of workers, such as youth. As Gramlich has pointed out, most below-minimum-wage workers are adults, and a large share of youths receive wages well above the minimum.

An even more serious weakness is the lack of data on the average wage of low-skill workers generally, let alone for a particular youth group. One approach might be to assume that low-skill workers are all at the previous minimum. Then the difference between two successive minimums reflects their wage increase, and deflating by the average wage expresses this as a relative change in minimum wage, or $(M_1 - M_0)/W$. This would not take account, of course, of any workers with wages between the two minimums. More serious, it cannot take into account the initial application of a minimum to a newly covered group of workers. In this case, the initial legal minimum is zero, and this measure becomes no different from the relative minimum. Both imply that a newly covered group is raised from a zero wage, and this is a flaw that gives excess weight to a coverage ratio.

Still another weakness of a relative minimum, or of a relative change in the minimum, is that the impact of a minimum on costs is assumed to rise in proportion to the rate increase. Both Gramlich and Welch have noted that the cost impact rises more than proportionately to the minimum-wage rate increase. Welch has developed still another relative minimum-wage measure to take account of this simply by squaring the minimum-wage rate, or $M^2C/W$. He calls this an index of the "potential effect" of a minimum wage "devoid of any sub-

FIGURE 6
MINIMUM-WAGE POTENTIAL INDEX, 1947–1979

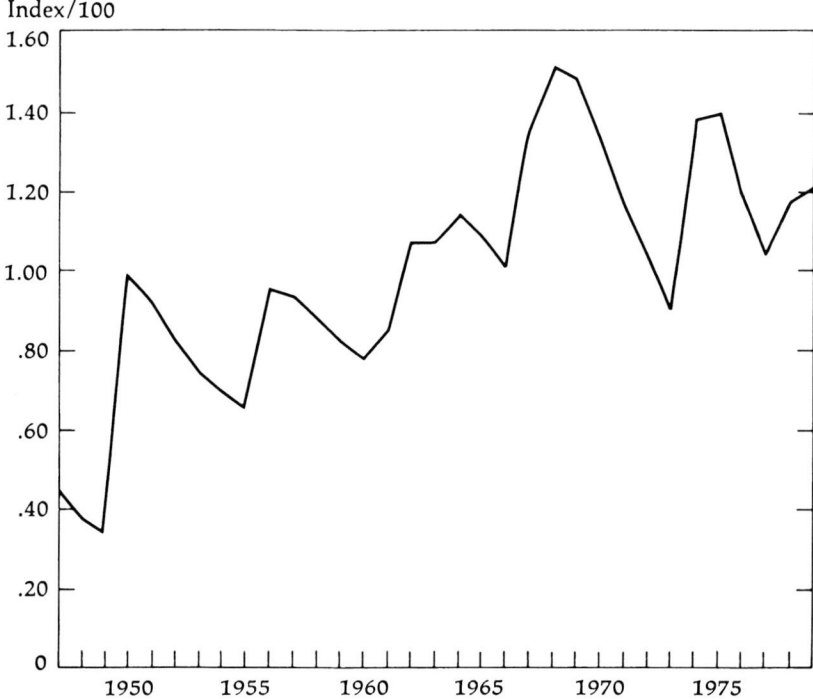

SOURCE: See appendix table 14.

sequent response."[5] The historical pattern of Welch's minimum-wage potential index also has a saw-toothed fluctuation around a rising trend, with an even more pronounced peak in 1968, as shown in figure 6.

## Weaknesses of the Conventional Measure

In spite of these efforts at modification, the commonly used measure remains the coverage-weighted relative minimum as developed by the BLS. This measure has significant weaknesses that are worth listing in summary.

The first of these, already mentioned, is the time trend in the historical pattern. This makes it more difficult to isolate minimum-

[5] Finis Welch, *Minimum Wages: Issues and Evidence* (Washington, D.C.: American Enterprise Institute, 1978), p. 8.

14

wage effects from other variables with correlated time trends.

A second problem lies in its coverage weighting. As already mentioned, Welch and Gramlich have argued for a more than proportionate effect from increased coverage. But the more important reason is not given: the pre-minimum-wage average wage in the uncovered sector is likely to be lower than in the covered sector.

A third problem is that a change in the minimum-wage rate alone is assumed to be a proxy for a change in the average wage of below-minimum workers. This assumption arises from the basic difficulty of having no estimate of the pre-minimum-wage equilibrium wage for workers below the minimum. It is presumed that for step increases in an existing minimum, the average wage of affected workers increases from one minimum to another. With any distribution of workers at wage rates between the two minimums, however, the average wage of below-minimum workers will exceed the previous minimum, $m_1 < \overline{w}_2 < m_2$; so a minimum-to-minimum increase will overstate the imposed wage increase. More important, the assumption ignores the implication of expressing the wage increase imposed by an initial legal minimum for newly covered workers as an increase from a previous legal level of zero.

A fourth problem is that the relative number of workers at below-minimum wages is not taken into account. It is not enough to measure the percentage of wage increase imposed on low-skill workers. The size of the low-skill group affects the ease of inter-worker substitution. It also affects the labor cost increase, the inter-factor substitution, and the price and output effects on the firm. That is, the minimum wage places a pressure on the labor costs of the firm, which cannot be identified without taking into account the proportion of workers affected by the imposed wage increase.[6]

A fifth problem, closely related, is that the proportion of below-minimum workers must increase as the minimum is set at higher levels. Thus, there is a multiplicative relation between the minimum and this proportion, and both increase together. This disproportionate effect also works in the opposite direction for erosion of the minimum's effectiveness when independent forces raise the wage distribution. The impact falls faster than the average wage increase. Thus, the commonly used measure may not show steep enough fluctuations up or down.

[6] For the elasticity measure, the same group of workers should be referred to in the numerator and the denominator. Either the percentage change in low-wage-worker employment is divided by the percentage change in their wage increase, or the percentage change in total employment is divided by the percentage change in average wage for all workers.

15

FIGURE 7

## SHIFTS IN INDUSTRY WEIGHTS IN THE BLS MEASURE, 1950–1978

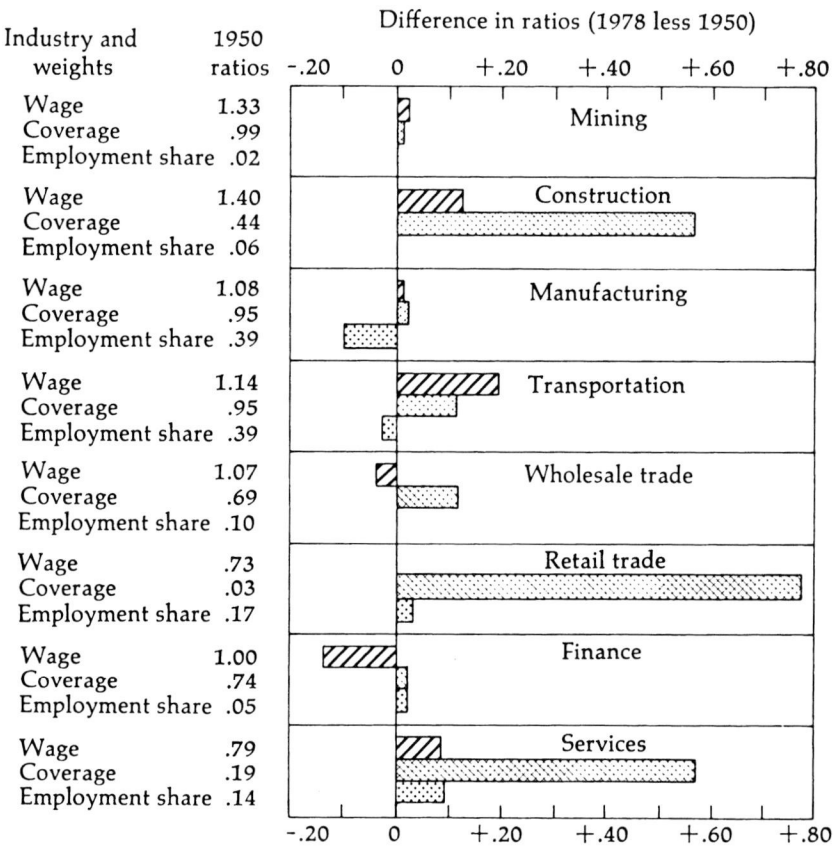

SOURCE: See appendix table 16.

A sixth weakness of the BLS measure is that the current shifting of its average wage, coverage ratio, and employment weights tends to incorporate into the measure itself some of its effects. If the minimum causes wage decreases in uncovered jobs, the average wage used as a deflator in the minimum-wage measure is affected. If disemployment occurs in covered jobs while increased employment occurs in uncovered jobs, the coverage ratio is affected. Finally, the employment weights among industries are affected if employment trends are slowed in the more completely covered parts of each industry or in the more affected industries. So the causative variable is being affected by feedbacks from its own effects.

These feedbacks may be small, but there is evidence of their existence in the worksheet data to compile the BLS measure, as shown in figure 7. The coverage ratio for the basic covered sector declined until 1967, when some newly covered jobs were lumped into it. A further slight decline in basic coverage had occurred by 1974. The employment share weights by industry group decreased from 1950 to 1978 in the four industries most completely covered initially—mining, transportation, manufacturing, and wholesale trade. The employment share increased in the services industry and retail trade, which had the least coverage initially. Most of this gain occurred in 1967, when their coverage was sharply increased. The relative wage increased substantially only in services and construction, both of which had substantial coverage increases in 1967 and 1974.

Of course, the bulk of these shifts may be due to independent forces, but they do correspond to the direction of effects expected from higher minimums and increased coverage. The intercorrelations involved make the minimum-wage effects more difficult to isolate and distort both the minimum-wage coefficient in regressions and the elasticity measure.

# 3
# A New Minimum-Wage Measure

The Labor Department's traditional approach to measuring minimum-wage effects always had two elements that now seem worth more consideration. One is the identification of a pure measure of the wage increase "required" by any new minimum-wage rate before the data are commingled with subsequent adjustments. The other is the use of estimated wage distributions to calculate that required wage increase.

## Defining the Minimum-Wage Impact

**First- and Second-Order Effects.** Minimum-wage legislation, of course, does not require that any particular workers be paid a minimum wage but only that those workers who are employed after the effective date be paid at least such a rate. Employers immediately make some adjustments to that requirement; other adjustments take more time to put into effect. One of the immediate adjustments is the hiring of fewer workers in the types of jobs previously compensated at below-minimum rates, which immediately affects the average wage and the number employed.

These effects create a measurement problem in using time series data to isolate minimum-wage effects where the minimum-wage measure is weighted by current employment coverage and divided by the current wage average. Some of the adjustments are fed back into the measure of what gave them their impetus. The minimum variable is thus distorted even before influences of other independent variables are considered.

The remedy would seem to be to use data in effect just before the effective date of a new minimum-wage requirement, not only wage data but also data on coverage ratio and employment weights. For a series of minimum-wage rate increases, it may be necessary to take account of the independently shifting wage and employment conditions under which new rates are applied. But the data base for calculating the minimum-wage measure in each period should be from a period before the one in which that minimum is being applied.

What we desire to measure, therefore, is what Welch has called the "potential effect . . . devoid of any subsequent response." If we refer to this as the minimum-wage impact, or first-order wage effect, we can turn to identifying more clearly the second-order effects of the minimum wage on both average wages and employment. It is important to realize that a number of conflicting directions of changes are included in the second-order effects. These are worth listing.

Among the second-order wage effects is, first, the "substitution" effect, in which the average wage is raised as a result of a shift in the composition of the labor force—there being a selective disemployment of low-wage workers and perhaps an increased employment of some types of high-wage workers. Second is the "ripple" effect, in which the wage rate of some workers is raised just above the minimum to maintain skill differentials or morale. Third is the "competitive" effect, which involves wage increases in other firms in the industry due either to union bargaining no longer restrained by competition from low-wage firms or to higher wage bidding for the now more demanded high-skill workers. The fourth, the "crowding" effect, lowers the average wage in uncovered jobs because of the increased supply of low-skill workers created by their disemployment in covered jobs.

The combined second-order wage effects, sometimes called the indirect wage effects, may be substantial, although they may be difficult to isolate empirically. Gramlich's separate wage regression suggested an overall minimum-related wage increase about twice the size of the percentage increase in the basic minimum-wage rate in 1974. Both, of course, were extremely small, and Gramlich's use of only an unweighted basic minimum-wage measure did not necessarily account for all of the minimum-wage impact.

Among the second-order employment effects is, first, the "worker substitution" effect, which selectively reduces employment of low-skill workers while increasing employment in some high-skill occupations. Second is the "factor substitution" effect, which reduces employment with labor-saving equipment or substitution of other inputs for labor generally. The third, the "competitive" effect, decreases employment in low-wage firms while increasing employment in high-wage firms of the same industries. The fourth, the "product substitution" effect, tends to shift consumer demand among industries because of higher costs and prices in the most affected industries. The fifth, the "crowding" effect, increases employment in uncovered jobs and industries.

The negative direction of employment changes must logically predominate in order for second-order adjustments within firms to be cost-saving and because gains elsewhere will not exceed the losses. The overall decrease, however, will be less severe than the decreases among the most affected industries, firms, and workers. This suggests the importance in time series studies of trying to disaggregate the data into more affected and less affected categories in order to detect the distribution of effects.

**A Minimum-Wage-Impact Formula.** The Labor Department traditionally has used wage-distribution survey data in effect just before the effective date of a new minimum to calculate the amount of wage increase that would be required to raise all below-minimum rates to the minimum. This first-order wage effect will be referred to hereafter simply as the minimum-wage impact. There are two levels, however, of this minimum-wage impact—the impact on the average wage of the below-minimum workers and the impact on the average wage of all workers.

The minimum-wage impact on the average wage of below-minimum workers is simply the difference between the minimum and their preminimum average wage: $(M - w) = \Delta w$. This must be positive since the wage average here is defined as a below-minimum average. Any negative difference is treated as zero, or as having no impact. Multiplying by 100 and dividing by the preminimum wage shows the percentage increase required for low-wage workers: $100(M - w)/w = \Delta w\%$.

The minimum-wage impact on the average wage of all workers may be calculated, first, by multiplying the hourly wage rate increase for below-minimum workers $(M - w)$ by their number $(e)$ and by their average weekly hours $(h)$. This gives the required weekly payroll increase for below-minimum workers. Multiplying this increase by 100 and dividing by the preminimum total weekly payroll of all workers $(EHW)$ gives the percentage increase required in total weekly payroll: $100(M - w)eh/EHW$. This is the same as the percentage increase required in the overall average wage. It also may be computed as 100 times the wage increase of below-minimum workers times their fraction of all workers divided by the overall average wage. Letting $e/E = z$, this becomes: $100(M - w)z/W$.

Of course, the coverage ratio $(C)$, which is less than unity, must reduce the required percentage increase in the average wage of an industry; so the coverage-weighted measure becomes: $100(M - w)zC/W$. Since this is a pure measure of the first-order wage effect for a covered sector of the industry, there is no need to modify it to take account of the second-order effect in an uncovered sector, as with the ratio $C/(1 - C)$. The wage increase and the coverage ratio, however, must apply to the same group of below-minimum workers. To separate the effect of a minimum-wage increase for an existing coverage group from the effect of an increase in coverage to a newly covered group requires a computation for two separate groups and their summation.

When two different minimums with two different coverage groups are identified, such as for basic and newly covered workers ($M_b$, $M_n$, and $C_b$, $C_n$), two separate calculations of minimum-wage impacts can be summed together, as in the BLS mesure. Two separate proportions of below-minimum workers ($z_b$, $z_n$) and two separate below-minimum wage averages ($w_b$, $w_n$) are also needed. Thus, the formula for the percentage increase in the average wage required is: $100[(M_b - w_b)z_b C_b + (M_n - w_n)z_n C_n]/W$. This may be referred to as the relative minimum-wage impact for an industry ($i$) or $(MI/W)_i$.

When data are available separately by industry, an additional employment weighting procedure can be used to combine them into an all-industry average or overall minimum-wage-impact measure. Again, the proper data needed include not only the employment share, the average wage, and the coverage ratio for each industry ($E_i/E$, $W_i$, $C_i$) but also separate industry data on the below-minimum wage averages and proportions of workers for two coverage groups ($w_{bi}$, $z_{bi}$, $w_{ni}$, $z_{ni}$). This obviously was not done in the commonly used BLS measure. Thus, the overall relative minimum-wage-impact formula becomes: $100 \Sigma (E_i/E)[(M_b - w_b)z_b C_b + (M_n - w_n)z C_n]/W_i = MI/W$.

### Data for a Measure

**Labor Department Estimates.** The Labor Department has published estimates of the number of workers receiving less than the minimum wages in 1950 and 1956 and of the proportion of covered workers they represented. Since 1961 it has published such estimates for each minimum-wage level in its annual reports.[1] With these numbers they have estimated the "annual wage bill increase required" to raise these workers to each minimum, as well as the "percent of covered payrolls" represented by this increase. Breakdowns of these estimates have been provided for each separate type of minimum. Unfortunately, breakdowns have not been presented by separate industry groups,

---

[1] These data are published in the January annual reports to Congress by the secretary of labor, as required by section 4(d) of the Fair Labor Standards Act, 1961 amendment. See U.S. Department of Labor, Employment Standards Administration, *Minimum Wage and Maximum Hours Standards under the Fair Labor Standards Act* (yearly).

and the Employment Standards Administration has no past records readily available by industry. Only the coverage ratios for the basic covered and newly covered minimums have been published separately by industry.

One outstanding fact revealed by these estimates, as shown in figure 8, is the small magnitude of minimum-wage impacts. The highest percentage increase in payrolls required by the basic minimum wage was the 1.1 percent in 1968. Somewhat larger percentage increases occurred for some newly covered groups, but these minimums covered a small fraction of all workers.

Another characteristic of these estimated minimum-wage impacts is that they have quite a different time pattern from measures that have been used in regression studies of effects. For the basic minimum, neither the real minimum-wage measure nor the relative minimum-wage measure shows quite as pronounced a peak in 1968 as the percentage increases in payrolls. Furthermore, the BLS measure of the coverage-weighted relative minimum had an upward trend. In contrast, the percentage increases in payrolls show declining trends, after 1968 for the basic minimum and after 1960 for the minimums for the newly covered workers (excluding farm, government, and household service workers). Only the increase in coverage accompanying the minimums for the newly covered workers would raise the later levels of a combined measure somewhat, and most of this increase occurred in the middle periods, in 1961 and in 1967.

One piece of information that can be derived from these estimates is the implied straight-time average wage rates—both the average wage for below-minimum covered workers and the average wage for all covered workers—just before each minimum-wage increase. The only additional information needed to derive these wage averages is the average weekly hours, and averages published in prior years may be used here. Thus, with these implied wage averages, all of the elements of a minimum-wage-impact measure are obtainable from the Labor Department's annual reports on minimum wages. Data are missing only in the years with no increase in minimum-wage rates or in years when increases occurred only in the basic rate or only in the rate for the newly covered sector. In these years, no $z$, $w$, or $W$ is available. So estimates must be made from some other published wage distribution data.

**The 1970 Wage Distribution.** Fortunately, the Labor Department has published the wage distribution in April 1970 for all private nonfarm industries with breakdowns by coverage groups under the federal

# FIGURE 8

## Percentage Increases in Payroll Required by Minimum Wages, 1950–1979

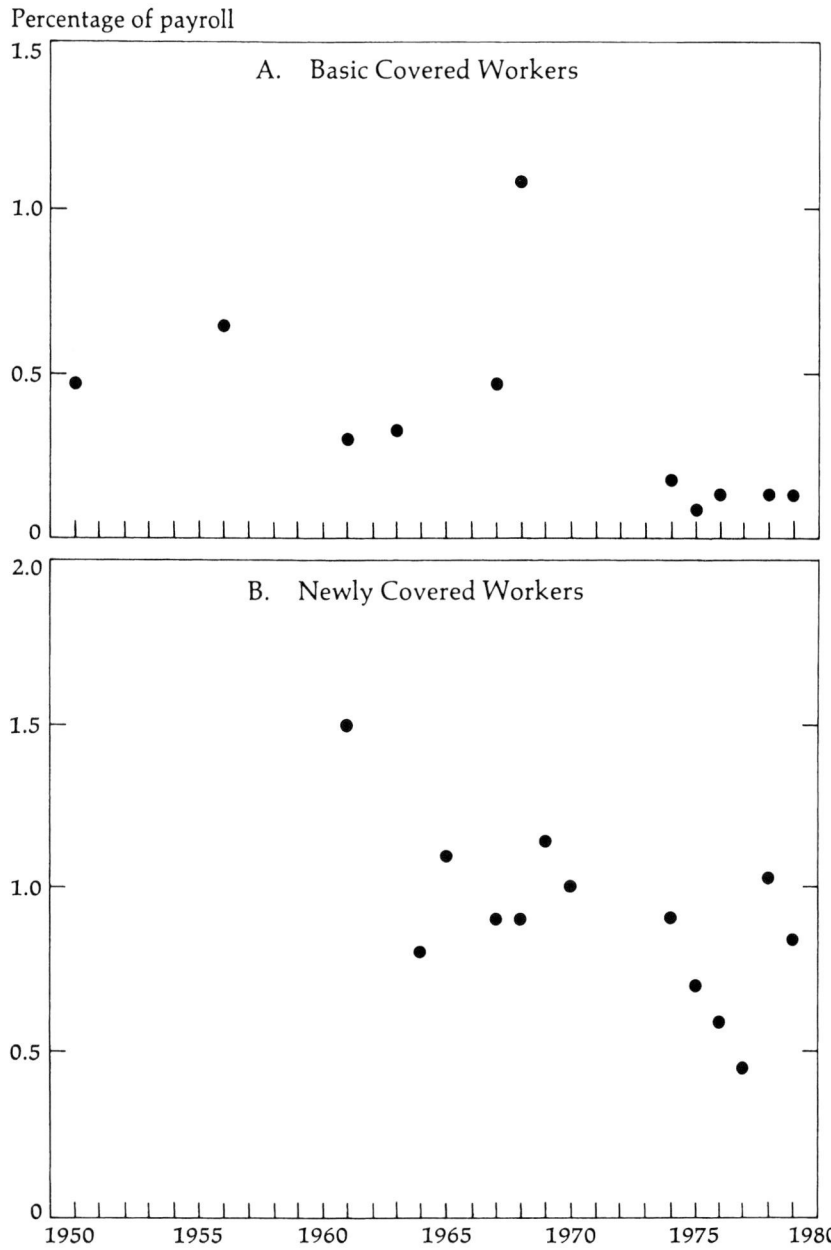

Percentage of payroll

A. Basic Covered Workers

B. Newly Covered Workers

Source: See appendix table 17.

## FIGURE 9

### WAGE DISTRIBUTION BY COVERAGE STATUS, APRIL 1970

Cumulative percentage of workers

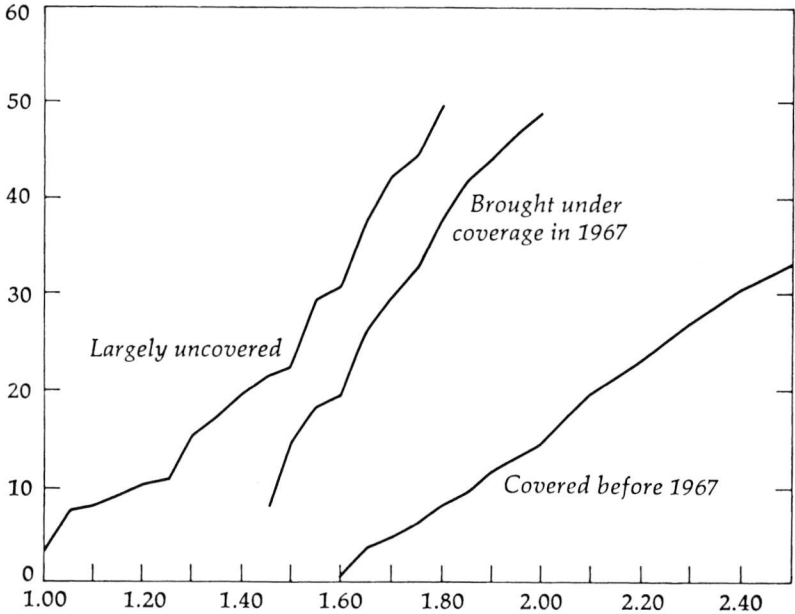

SOURCE: See appendix table 18.

minimums.[2] For $0.05 intervals ($0.10 intervals above $2), it shows the cumulative percentage of all workers below each wage level. Three separate distributions are shown; basic covered jobs, with a minimum of $1.60 (before 1966 amendments), newly covered jobs, with a minimum of $1.45, and uncovered jobs. For each coverage group there also are separate distributions by geographic region and by metropolitan and nonmetropolitan area. There are also separate wage distributions by major industry division for the jobs under the basic covered minimum and by the two industry divisions most affected by the minimum wage for newly covered workers, retail trade and services.

One characteristic of these distributions is that when plotted on a graph they show an almost straight-line pattern, as shown in figure 9. This is especially so if the distributions are for only the lower half of

[2] U.S. Department of Labor, Employment Standards Administration, *Wages and Hours of Nonsupervisory Employees in All Private Nonagricultural Industries by Coverage Status under the Fair Labor Standards Act* (1972).

## FIGURE 10
### RELATIVE WAGE DISTRIBUTION BY COVERAGE STATUS, APRIL 1970

Cumulative percentage of workers

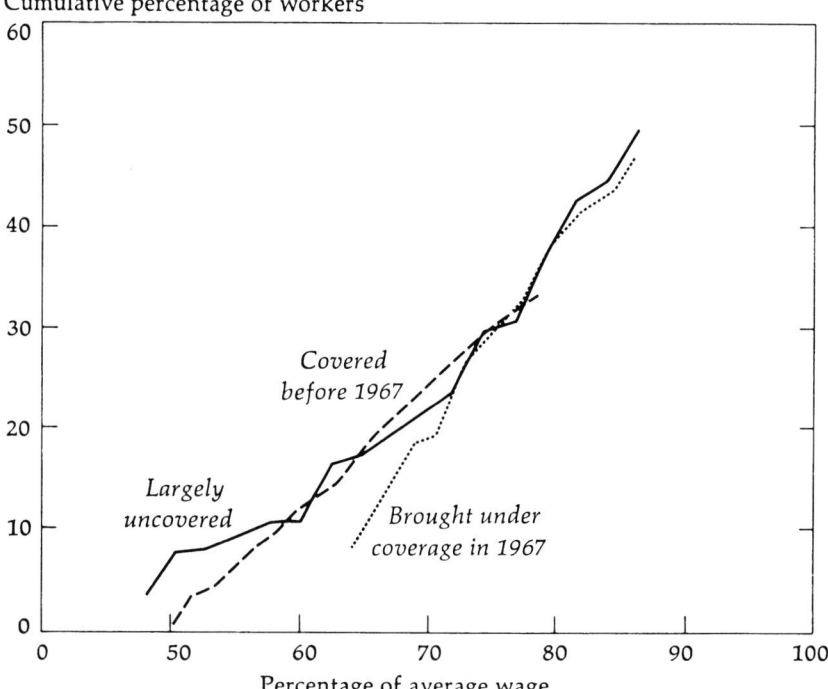

Percentage of average wage

SOURCE: See appendix table 18.

all workers. It should be noted that for the lower half there is little evidence of an S-shape related to a normal distribution such as Welch used in his hypothetical illustration. For his inference of more than proportionate impact, it was only necessary that the cumulative distribution be rising, with a multiplicative effect on the impact.

Furthermore, if the distributions by coverage group are standardized by expressing the wage levels as a percentage of the average wage of the group, the lines for the three groups tend to coincide, as shown in figure 10. They diverge most widely among the lowest 10 or 20 percent of workers. The newly covered jobs are pushed to the right toward higher wages, steepening the slope, while the uncovered jobs are trailing to the left toward lower wages, flattening the slope. The former would be consistent with some bunching at the $1.45 minimum in the newly covered group without noticeable ripple effect, and the latter is consistent with crowding in the uncovered group below the $1.45 minimum.

25

# FIGURE 11
## LINEAR WAGE DISTRIBUTION MODEL

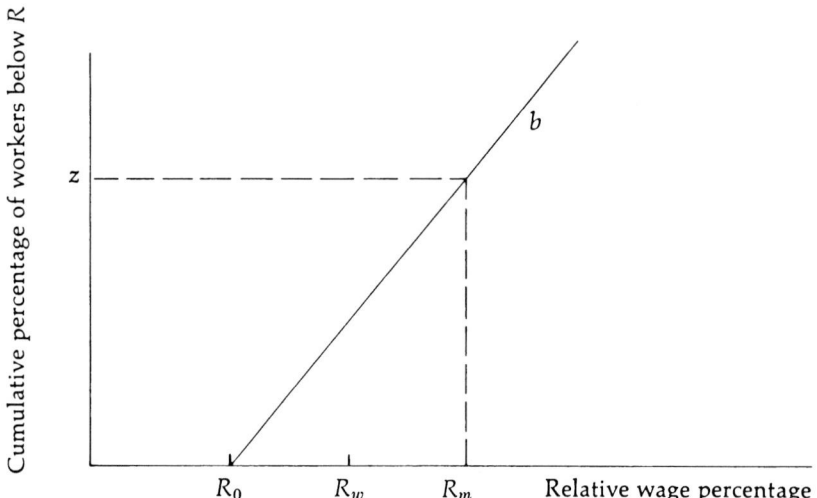

SOURCE: Author.

**A Model Wage Distribution.** A linear wage distribution, then, provides a simple model for interpolating data for the missing years in the Labor Department estimates and perhaps for using a wage distribution to make industry estimates. The model assumes that the linear distribution is constant over time—that is, that independent forces affecting the average wage cause the same percentage increases in wages at all wage levels. This assumption also is implicit in most time series regression studies of minimums.[3]

The time-constant linear wage distribution may be represented on a graph as a positively sloped straight line, as shown in figure 11. The horizontal axis of the graph shows relative wage levels, or the ratio of any wage level to the average wage, which is expressed as a percentage: $100w/W = R$. The vertical axis is the cumulative percentage of workers at or below the relative wage level ($z$). For any given minimum-wage rate ($M$), there is a corresponding relative wage level ($R_m$) and percentage of workers ($z$). A zero value of $z$ occurs at some relative wage ($R_0$) that indicates the relative wage below which

---

[3] This assumption, of course, can be tested empirically. The linear parameters implied by the Labor Department estimates showed shifts, which may have been due partly to shifting weights and partly to cyclical tightening and slackening of labor markets.

there are no workers and thus below which a minimum wage would be ineffective. A point halfway between $R_m$ and $R_0$ indicates the relative wage average for workers below the minimum.

Now, with this model, a conceptual separation can be made between two opposite effects: raising the minimum-wage rate and increasing the average wage. At a given average wage, a raise in the minimum-wage rate moves $R_m$ to the right along the straight line, thus raising $z$ and $R_w$. At a given minimum-wage rate, an increase in the average wage moves $R_m$ to the left along the straight line, thus lowering $z$ and $R_w$. If the average wage increases far enough, it will move $R_m$ below $R_0$, making the minimum wage ineffective.

## Computing the Minimum-Wage Impact

**An Overall Measure.** Using this model, a new annual measure of overall minimum-wage impact can be constructed that interpolates missing values for years between increases in the minimum in the Labor Department estimates in annual reports on minimum wages. This is done in two steps. First, for years in which the minimum is raised, the published data provide $R_m$ and $R_w$, which can be used to derive the parameter $R_0$: $(R_m - R_w)2 - R_m = R_0$. The published figure for $z$ can be used to derive the slope parameter: $z/(R_m - R_0) = b$. This gives two points determining the implied linear wage distribution. Separate data and coverage rates are available for two different minimum-wage rates; so separate computations can be carried out and then summed. Second, for years between increases (with $M$ constant), $R_m$ can be computed using the published average hourly earnings series to obtain the average wage. $R_m$ is then applied to the previous parameters, $R_0$ and $b$, to obtain estimates of $R_w$, $w$, and $z$. These, in turn, can be used in the general formula to compute the minimum-wage impact for each minimum-wage rate and then combined. Such a computation can provide an annual measure of relative minimum-wage impact for all private nonfarm industries.[4] Unfortunately, detail is not available to provide a breakdown of this measure for separate industries.

One inherent characteristic of the measure in this form should be noted. The Labor Department has provided new estimates for each step rise in the minimum-wage rates. This not only shifts the weights for coverage and employment and changes the average wage for payroll calculations but also shifts the wage distribution parameters.

[4] The required wage increase can also be expressed as a percentage of the average wage of below-minimum workers, and elasticities can be computed for this group.

These parameter shifts may provide an item of separate study interest, but it might have been preferable to hold them constant for some longer period. The point is that the measure in this form still allows considerable feedback of effects on the measure of impact.

**An Industry-Weighted Measure.** Since the 1970 published wage distribution also provided breakdowns by major industry division, it is possible to use them to construct a minimum-wage impact measure for each industry. First, regression estimates can be made of the $R_0$ and $b$ parameters of these 1970 distributions for each industry (see table 19, in the appendix). Separate regressions can be run for basic and newly covered jobs in retail trade and services. These parameters, available only once, are assumed constant for all years studied. Second, a prior-month average wage is available from published data for each industry (using estimates for years before 1966). Dividing the industry wage by the two minimums gives the $R_m$ for each. Third, the $R_m$s can be applied to the $R_0$ and $b$ parameters to compute impacts for each minimum, and the impacts can be summed. Dividing by the prior-month wage gives the relative minimum-wage impact on the industry.

An alternative measure can now be constructed for all private nonfarm industries by employment-weighting these separate industry measures. This industry-weighted minimum-wage-impact measure should be similar to the "overall" minimum-wage-impact measure computed from the Labor Department's annual reports on minimum wages. The measures may diverge, however, to the extent that the Labor Department's overall estimates involved both shifting weights and shifting parameters of the wage distributions. The alternative has the advantage of permitting some construction of a measure for subindustries where no other Labor Department estimates are available.

Further explanation is needed here on three aspects of the construction of both forms of the minimum-wage-impact measures in this study. The first is the use of constant weights. To measure a pure first-order wage effect, it is important to hold constant any coverage and employment weights so that there is no feedback of second-order adjustments on the measure itself. Since independent changes over time also occur in coverage and employment, it may not be appropriate to hold the weights constant indefinitely. As a compromise, this study holds constant the coverage and employment weights for the duration of each amendment period. This treats each amendment as an autonomous act of legislation and lets the effects of subsequent programmed step increases be studied as part of that initial act.

A second aspect of the construction concerns the use of a prior-month wage. Since average wages rise continuously and would deflate the relative minimum-wage impact accordingly, there is a question of how long to hold the measure constant. Other time series regression studies using monthly or quarterly data have tried lags on the minimum-wage measure of up to twenty-four months but have found most effects to occur in the first quarter and to be pretty well exhausted within a year. Legislated step increases have also used twelve-month intervals following the initial effective date. For this study, therefore, the relative minimum-wage impact is computed with a constant wage for successive twelve-month intervals following the initial prior month. This keeps the impact measure constant for twelve-month intervals during which its effects are presumed to be occurring. The independent changes in wage are presumed to shift the wage distribution with a lag at evenly spaced intervals.

The third aspect is due to the choice of annual data for this study. In other studies using the conventional coverage-weighted relative minimum annually, an average of the two applicable rates is computed whenever a minimum is raised within a calendar year. This occurred in fourteen of the thirty-three years. Since this study holds the wage and minimum-wage impact constant for twelve months at a time, this annual averaging procedure is continued for every year until 1975, when the first of January became the effective date. This averaging both reduces and delays some of the peaks in the measure in the annual data.

**Time Patterns.** The results of computing the new measures of the relative minimum-wage impact may now be examined for their time patterns, as shown in figure 12. Several characteristics distinguish them from other measures that have been used in time series regressions. First, the magnitude of the relative minimum-wage impact is very small. This might be expected from the small percentage increases in payrolls published by the Labor Department. In the overall form, the new measure never quite reaches 1 percent, even in the 1968 peak. In the industry-weighted form, the new measure is somewhat smaller.[5] Both measures, in fact, are about two decimals smaller

---

[5] The industry-weighted form could have been raised closer to the overall form by computing each industry's $R_u$ parameter at three standard deviations above the regression line instead of two standard deviations, but this would have produced a 1970 estimate greater than the survey data for that benchmark year.

## FIGURE 12
### Relative Minimum-Wage Impact (Two Forms), 1947–1979

Percentage of wage

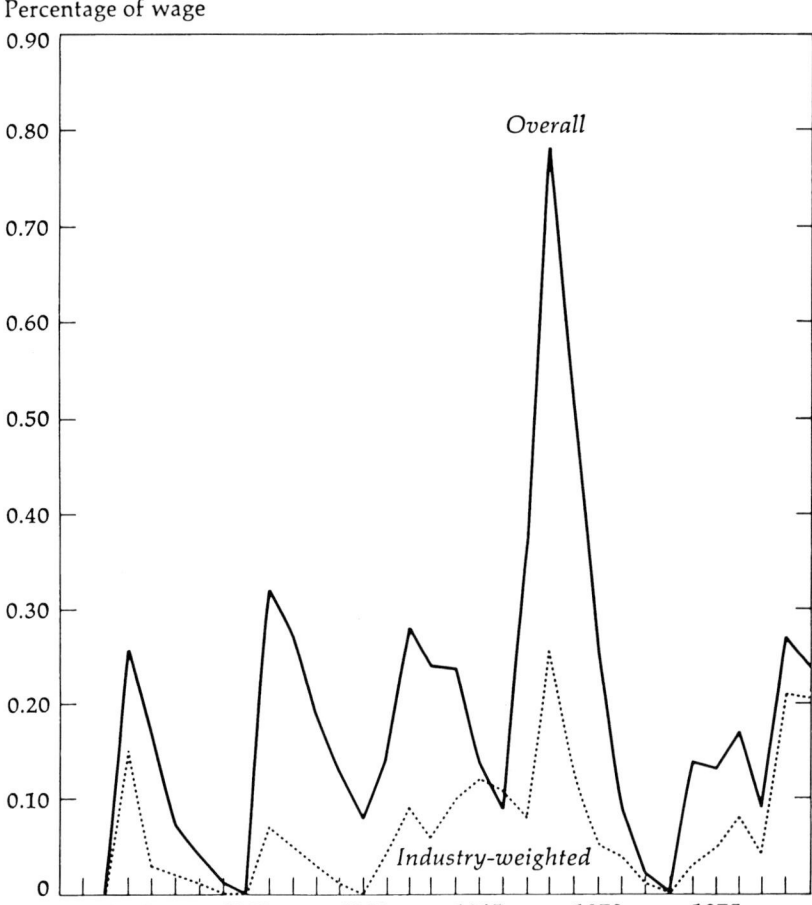

Source: See appendix table 21.

than the conventional measure, since they are expressed in percentages, while the conventional measure is a ratio.

Second, the relative minimum-wage-impact measures drop to about zero in 1955 and 1973 and have virtually no time trend. Thus, they indicate when wage inflation has made the federal minimums ineffective. More important, they show for industry subgroups when the wage is too high to have any direct effect. In the overall form the correlation with time is $r = .270$, and in the industry-weighted form it is $r = .426$. This contrasts with the strong upward trend in the conventional coverage-weighted relative minimum wage, with a time correlation of $r = .878$. Both of these considerations make it more difficult in time series regressions using the conventional measures to separate the effects of the minimum from the influence of other independently rising variables and may bias the coefficient of the minimum-wage measure toward zero or the wrong sign.

Third, there is a wider range of fluctuation in this measure than in others. The range is 4.4 times the mean in the overall form and 4.0 times the mean in the industry-weighted form. This compares with 0.74 in the coverage-weighted relative minimum, and most of that range is produced by the upward trend. This is important in time series regression studies because the extreme values are emphasized by squaring the deviations from the mean.[6]

Fourth, the severity of different amendments and the turning points in yearly changes differ from those of other measures and differ somewhat between the two forms of the new measure. As in the Welch index, the extreme peak is in 1968. The overall form shows about the same magnitude of peaks in 1950, 1956, 1962, and 1978, while the industry-weighted form shows stronger peaks in both 1950 and 1978. The upward time trend in other measures tends to produce successively larger peaks, although the largest percentage changes occur in 1967 and 1950. The latter is of special interest because many studies using household survey data have started with 1954 and thus miss this largest minimum-wage change. The overall form of the new measure also departs from other measures in certain turning points. It delays its 1961 upturn until 1962, fails to show a second peak in 1964, and shows a decline in 1975. The industry-weighted form conforms to the other measures in its turns except that it peaks in 1965 and is declining in 1967.

**Forms for Testing.** Quite possibly these differences in measures may not handicap time series regression studies very seriously. As indexes of minimum-wage impacts, slightly different measures may behave similarly enough to reveal the larger effects in any subgroup that is most affected. In cases where the minimum-wage effects are hard to isolate, however, such small differences may be important. The differences also raise doubts about the accuracy of present methods of measuring minimum-wage impacts, and they may help explain some of the diversity in elasticity measures that has resulted.

---

[6] The sharper fluctuations in the new measure reflect the multiplier effect of the increasing proportion of workers below the minimum wage as the minimum-wage level is raised. Table 20, in the appendix, compares how the different minimum measures rise with a rate increase.

While the new measures may be a step in the right direction, the differences between them do not lend confidence to their accuracy. Many of their differences, however, lie in the combining of industry measures into a single all-industry measure. For single-industry studies of minimum-wage effects, any overall minimum-wage measure may not be appropriate. This is where the linear models using industry parameter estimates are needed.

For this study both forms of the relative minimum-wage impact were tested with all private nonfarm data, and the industry-weighted form worked better. In any event, since the industry parameters had to be used for the separate industry regressions, it seemed better to start with the industry-weighted form with the all-industry regressions.

For empirical testing purposes, it also seemed advisable to use a comparable construction of the coverage-weighted relative minimum. So this conventional measure was adjusted by using the prior-month wage, the twelve-month intervals and annual averaging, and the constant coverage and employment weights for each amendment period. Computation of this adjustment showed that it did not substantially alter the conventional measure for all private nonfarm data, for the adjusted measure has a high correlation ($r = .988$) with its usual form. It also worked better in regressions for all private nonfarm data. So, throughout this study, $MC/W$ is in this comparable adjusted form, and $MI/W$ is based on the industry parameters.[7]

---

[7] See table 21, in the appendix, for the annual data on these measures for all private nonfarm industries.

# 4
## Effects among Major Industry Divisions

The focus of recent attention in minimum-wage studies has shifted away from industries and toward worker groups. This is due in part to the social reform objective of the legislation, which is aimed at helping the low-income worker, and in part to the opportunities provided by available statistical data. From the beginning it was recognized that the impact of a legal minimum wage would fall unequally on the lowest-wage industries, and the early studies were aimed at collecting data and analyzing the effects on these industries. To the extent that the burdens of regulation were perceived to fall on "bad" employers, public opinion was little concerned with these studies. Economists, however, pointed out that the burden of disemployment effects might also fall on the most disadvantaged workers—youth, females, and blacks. By the mid-1960s there was growing social concern with the high unemployment experienced by these groups. It was then that a new statistical opportunity was realized for minimum-wage studies. The data collected since World War II by the Census Bureau surveys of sample households began to provide a long enough time series for regression analysis, and this data source provided national aggregate estimates of employment and unemployment for demographic subgroups. Accordingly there was a burst of regression studies of minimum-wage effects on youth, females, and blacks in the early 1970s.

There are some advantages, however, in continuing to study the minimum-wage effects on industries. In the first place, the employment of disadvantaged workers is heavily concentrated in the low-wage industries. This has been recognized in some studies by attempts to adjust the conventional minimum-wage measure, which allows for different coverage ratios by industry, with industry employment weights that use data on the distribution of youth employment by industry. It would seem that such adjustments should be accompanied by efforts to take account, also, of industry differences in the independent variables affecting employment.

Second, man-hours measure the amount of labor hired more accurately than the number of workers employed. The Census Bureau's household surveys have collected data on the number of workers employed, and only since 1963 has a breakdown been available between rough categories of part-time and full-time workers— those working less or more than thirty-five hours a week. The Labor Department's industry data collected from employing establishments include both the number of workers and the average weekly hours worked, which may be multiplied to show aggregate weekly man-hours of labor hired. Industry studies, therefore, should provide a more sensitive measure of the disemployment effects of a minimum wage and an indication of the industries in which part-time jobs are more affected.

Third, data on average hourly earnings are available by subindustry to provide a basis for comparing the size of the minimum-wage impact with employment changes. In the data collected from employing establishments, dividing payrolls by man-hours provides average hourly earnings for the same subgroups for which man-hours and employment are shown. Studies using the household survey data have not had a wage figure for each worker group whose employment changes were compared. Indirect information provides some ranking of groups by average wage, but the wage distributions are widely overlapping. Some of the problems of isolating minimum-wage effects for aggregated groups containing widely differing wage levels can be avoided in subindustry studies.

Finally, a longer historical series of detailed industry data is available than of household data. This is useful because each amendment to the minimum-wage law is like a separate social experiment. Each imposed certain initial rate increases with scheduled step increases that were effective for brief periods and then were gradually eroded by general wage inflation. Employers' adjustments may have been affected by expectations of the later increases. Thus, the early history of minimum-wage experience might be more critical. In any event, the largest percentage increase in the relative minimum wage was imposed in 1950. It is unfortunate, therefore, that most of the minimum-wage studies using household data have begun with 1954 or with 1963, for lack of earlier comparable detail.

Industry studies can thus provide information complementary to the studies of worker groups. As indicated in chapter 3, there are several kinds of second-order effects of a minimum wage on employment. The substitutions among types of workers may be among the most significant effects, and these may not show up in industry studies. Competitive effects among firms in the same industry may also require the detailed data that were available only in the earlier minimum-wage studies. Regression studies of subindustry totals, however, may shed considerable light on where in the economy the greatest effects have occurred. And this may have implications for the kinds of effects observed for disadvantaged workers. The better measures for industry studies and the greater and longer detail available may also provide opportunities for testing the minimum-wage measures and statistical methods used.

This study is designed to use the establishment data by industry to show any differences in results from using two different minimum-wage measures: (1) the conventional measure, or the coverage-weighted relative minimum with adjusted construction, and (2) the new proposed measure, or the relative minimum-wage impact. The study is also designed to illustrate the importance of disaggregating to subindustry groups to reveal the extent and distribution of minimum-wage effects. There are some industries as well as some worker groups that bear most of the burden of disemployment. Others, in higher-wage groups, may gain somewhat from the minimum wage, and their employment changes from independent causes may cover up the disemployment effects in the aggregate. The approach of the study will be limited, however, to a rather simple and uniform application of variables to various industries. Unfortunately, as industries are disaggregated, more variables and more varied equations and methods may be needed to isolate the minimum from independent influences that can be included in the scope of this study. Yet it is expected that even a uniform approach will show greater disemployment effects for those industries on which a minimum wage has a greater impact.

## Effects for All Industries

The effect of a minimum wage on the national economy might be expected to be hard to detect, since the minimum-wage rates have historically been set rather low and there are many other dynamic influences on the economy. Nevertheless, there is considerable interest in the total effect, and it provides a starting point for comparison with industry subdivisions.

There are two major exclusions and one minor one to make in the economywide totals to be considered. First, government employment will be excluded as being primarily determined by political decisions rather than by private market decisions. Second, the agricultural sector of the economy will be excluded, since it is not included in the Labor Department's data series from reports from establishments.[1] Third, private household workers will also be excluded, since they are not regularly included in the establishment reports within the services industries group.[2] The economywide total employed figure, therefore, is for all private nonfarm industries; and the employment data are for production workers only rather than for all employees.

**Wage Effects.** Gramlich's study of minimum wages provided an estimate of the impact on the average wage for the private nonfarm sector.[3] Using household data on a quarterly basis for the 1954–1975 period, he specified a regression equation that determined the rate of change in wage in terms of the rate of change in the basic minimum-wage rate, an adjusted unemployment rate reciprocal, and the rate of change in a price index (the gross domestic product deflator). The minimum wage, he found, had a significant effect in raising the average wage. From other data, he estimated that only half of the increase in the average wage could be accounted for as a direct, first-order effect of the minimum. The other half was attributed to indirect effects on wages above the minimum.

Unfortunately, Gramlich's estimates will be difficult to check with the annual data chosen for use in this study. Wage changes may track more closely with price changes on a quarterly basis, although he used an Almon lag procedure to cumulate the price effects over seventeen quarters. His unemployment rate was adjusted to normalize it for certain demographic shifts that affected the actual rate.

Nevertheless, it was of interest for this study to start by running a somewhat similar equation with annual data from establishments. A change ratio for the wage was regressed on the change ratio for

---

[1] The negative employment effects on farm labor of the minimum wage have been shown using other data sources, however. See Bruce L. Gardner, "Minimum Wages and the Farm Labor Market," *American Journal of Agricultural Economics*, vol. 54, no. 3 (August 1972), pp. 473–76; Theodore F. Lianos, "Impact of Minimum Wages upon the Level and Composition of Agricultural Employment," *American Journal of Agricultural Economics*, vol. 54, no. 3 (August 1972), pp. 477–84; and H. F. Gallasch, Jr., and Bruce L. Gardner, "Schooling and the Agricultural Minimum Wage," *American Journal of Agricultural Economics*, vol. 60, no. 2 (May 1978), pp. 264–68.

[2] See Yale Brozen, "Minimum Wage Rates and Household Workers," *Journal of Law and Economics* (October 1962), pp. 103–9; and J. Peter Mattila, "The Effect of Extending Minimum Wages to Cover Household Maids," *Journal of Human Resources* (Summer 1973), pp. 365–82.

[3] Edward M. Gramlich, "Impact of Minimum Wages on Other Wages, Employment, and Family Incomes," *Brookings Papers on Economic Activity*, no. 2 (1976), table 5.

the basic minimum-wage rate, the actual unemployment rate reciprocal (for adult males), and the change ratio of prices—where a change
ratio is each year's value divided by the previous year's value. Unfortunately, the overall fit of this regression to the data was not as
close as for Gramlich's, and the minimum-wage coefficient was not
statistically significant for either the 1954–1975 period or the
1947–1979 period.

Examination of the data, however, suggested a modification of
the equation. While the change ratios for wages and prices had a
fairly close positive association for most years, there was much more
rapid price inflation than wage increases in 1974, 1975, and 1979.
Attempts to fit some lag in the wage-price relation did not help,
because it did not apply to most years and wages rose much faster
in 1953 and 1972. A consideration of the stagflation phenomenon in
the recessions of 1970 and 1974–1975 led to the idea that there
might be some historic break in the wage-price relation, with a different relation applying to the 1970s. This could be handled by
introducing into the regression equation two more variables: first,
a zero dummy that takes the value of one in years following 1969
and, second, a multiple of that dummy times the change ratio in
prices. These provide a different intercept and slope for the wage-
price relation after 1969.

The results of this regression are shown in table 1. The overall
fit is closer than that of Gramlich's, and each of the other independent
variables is significant. The new minimum-wage measure, the relative minimum-wage impact, had a significant positive effect on the
change in wages, but neither the basic minimum wage (used by
Gramlich) nor the conventional minimum-wage measure was significant.

While this regression shows a positive relation of higher minimums resulting in a higher average wage, the numbers are hard to
interpret for change ratios, especially since the conventional minimum is a ratio and the new minimum is a percentage to begin with.
In any event, the size of the effect is very small. For the basic
minimum-wage equation, a 10 percent increase in the basic minimum
wage, or $0.13 more than the $1.32 average for the period, would
bring a 0.09 percent increase in the average wage, or about one-
quarter of a cent on the $2.79 average for the period.

**Employment Effects.** Gramlich did not run a regression relating the
minimum to total employment because his focus was on the effects
for youth. He did show his results, however, for three worker

## TABLE 1
### Private Nonfarm Wage Effects, 1947–1979

| Dependent | Constant | Minimum-Wage Measures | Other Independent Variables | $R^2$ | Autoregressive (lag) | Correlation |
|---|---|---|---|---|---|---|
| $CWAG = .2645$ | | $+ .0093\ CMB$ (1.1) | $+ .0328\ UNR$ (1.9) $+ .7427\ CPRI$ (7.8) $+ .6582\ D69$ (4.5) $- .6177\ CPID$ (4.4) | .8881 | (4) | −.029 |
| $CWAG = .2219$ | | $+ .0443\ C(1 + MC/W)$ (1.1) | $+ .0326\ UNR$ (1.8) $+ .7506\ CPRI$ (7.9) $+ .6733\ D69$ (4.4) $- .6322\ CPID$ (4.3) | .8872 | (2) | −.060 |
| $CWAG = .2426$ | | $+ .0374\ C(1 + MI/W)$ (2.0)* | $+ .0380\ UNR$ (2.3) $+ .7359\ CPRI$ (8.1) $+ .7059\ D69$ (5.3) $- .6623\ CPID$ (5.1) | .8772 | (4) | .066 |

NOTES: Symbols for variables: $CWAG$ = change in average hourly earnings ($); $CMB$ = change in basic minimum-wage rate ($); $C(1 + MC/W)$ = change in coverage-weighted relative minimum wage (ratio); $C(1 + MI/W)$ = change in relative minimum-wage impact (percent); $UNR$ = reciprocal of adult male unemployment rate (percent); $CPRI$ = change in price index, the private business GDP deflator; $D69$ = zero dummy becoming 1 after 1969; $CPID = CPRI \times D69$. Change means the yearly value divided by the previous year's value. In parentheses are $t$-values, with significance percentages indicated for minimum-wage measures only.
* Significant at 10 percent level.

SOURCES: U.S. Department of Labor, Bureau of Labor Statistics, *Employment and Earnings, United States, 1909-78,* bulletin 1312-11, and monthly issues of *Employment and Earnings;* and U.S. Department of Commerce, *The National Income and Product Accounts* and monthly issues of *Survey of Current Business.*

groups making up the total: youth, adult males, and adult females.[4] The other independent variables in his equation were the real gross domestic product (GDP), time, and a labor-supply measure; and his minimum-wage measure was the basic minimum deflated by a price index (the GDP deflator) using a four-quarter Almon lag. The resulting minimum-wage coefficients all had the expected negative sign but were not statistically significant for any group. Thus, it can be presumed that the minimum-wage measure did not have a significant effect on total employment.

By using a breakdown of employment into full-time and part-time categories, however, Gramlich was able to show significant effects for youth and adult males. The minimum-wage coefficients for both groups had negative signs for full-time employment and positive signs for part-time employment. The minimum-wage coefficients for adult females had the opposite signs. This still leaves the overall effects in doubt.

Another study, by Jacob Mincer, might also be mentioned here, for it showed more significant employment effects among worker groups for a shorter period, 1954–1969, by quarter.[5] Mincer's regression equation used the ratio of employment to population as the dependent variable; the independent variables were the conventional minimum-wage measure, the unemployment rate, the armed forces share of the population, and time. While no relation was shown for total employment, negative coefficients resulted for the minimum-wage measure in all subgroups and significantly so for those likely to be most affected. Still, the largest group, the prime-aged males, did not show a significant negative effect; so the overall effect remains in doubt.

It is of some interest, therefore, to see what the total employment effects may be in this study, using annual data from establishments for all private nonfarm business for the period 1947–1979. The approach is to use a simple demand-side equation with the independent variables consisting of output (real GDP in private nonfarm business), productivity (for private nonfarm business), and time, as well as the two alternative minimum-wage measures ($MC/W$ and $MI/W$). The equations are run separately for number employed and for man-hours as the dependent variable. All equations are adjusted for autocorrelation, selecting enough lags to minimize the autoregressive correlation. The results are shown in table 2.

[4] Gramlich, "Impact of Minimum Wages," tables 6, 7, and 8.
[5] Jacob Mincer, "Unemployment Effects of Minimum Wages," *Journal of Political Economy*, supplement (August 1976), pp. S87–104.

## TABLE 2

### Private Nonfarm Employment and Man-Hour Effects, 1947–1979

| Dependent | Constant | Minimum-Wage Measures | Other Independent Variables | $R^2$ | Autoregressive (lag) | Correlation |
|---|---|---|---|---|---|---|
| $NEMP =$ | $28.30 +$ | $2.474\ MC/W +$ <br>$(0.9)$ | $.0526\ RGDP - .2541\ PROD - .1963\ TIME + .0012\ TSQ$ <br>$(\,9.8)\qquad (4.0)\qquad\qquad (1.7)\qquad\quad (0.4)$ | $.9902$ | $(4)$ | $.061$ |
| $NEMP =$ | $28.61 -$ | $2.090\ MI/W +$ <br>$(1.2)$ | $.0570\ RGDP - .2763\ PROD - .2028\ TIME - .0001\ TSQ$ <br>$(10.1)\qquad (4.4)\qquad\qquad (2.0)\qquad\quad (0.0)$ | $.9937$ | $(3)$ | $-.013$ |
| $MANH =$ | $921.4 +$ | $109.0\ MC/W +$ <br>$(1.1)$ | $2.327\ RGDP - 7.545\ PROD - 13.20\ TIME - .3023\ TSQ$ <br>$(11.8)\qquad (3.9)\qquad\qquad (4.2)\qquad\quad (3.5)$ | $.9945$ | $(4)$ | $.063$ |
| $MANH =$ | $911.7 -$ | $96.88\ MI/W +$ <br>$(1.8)**$ | $2.556\ RGDP - 8.667\ PROD - 13.95\ TIME - .3828\ TSQ$ <br>$(13.8)\qquad (4.8)\qquad\qquad (5.3)\qquad\quad (4.9)$ | $.9966$ | $(4)$ | $.037$ |

Notes: Symbols for variables: $NEMP$ = number of nonsupervisory workers employed (millions); $MANH$ = man-hours per week (millions); $MC/W$ = coverage-weighted relative minimum wage (ratio); $MI/W$ = relative minimum-wage impact (percent); $RGDP$ = real gross domestic product, private nonfarm business ($ billions); $PROD$ = productivity index, private nonfarm business; $TIME$ = year minus 1946; $TSQ$ = $TIME$ squared. In parentheses are $t$-values, with significance percentages indicated for minimum-wage measures only.

** Significant at 5 percent level.

Sources: Bureau of Labor Statistics, Employment and Earnings, United States, 1909–78, and monthly issues of Employment and Earnings; U.S. Department of Commerce, The National Income and monthly issues of Survey of Current Business; and Economic Report of the President, January 1980.

Using the conventional measure ($MC/W$), the coefficient fails to show the negative sign expected in theory, although it is not statistically significant. Using the new measure ($MI/W$), however, the expected negative sign occurs. It is not quite significant at the 10 percent confidence level when the number employed is the dependent variable, but it is significant at the 5 percent confidence level when man-hours is the dependent variable. The overall fit is closer for the man-hours equation, and the other independent variables are all significant.[6]

With this clear indication of a man-hour loss due to the minimum, there remains the question of its size. What would be the loss, say, for a 10 percent rise in minimum-wage rates around the mean values of this linear regression? This is complicated by the fact that the minimum-wage-impact measure rises faster than the minimum rate and that it has been computed as a weighted average among industries. The actual data in 1967 are close to the mean values, however, and the Labor Department's estimates for 1967 provide the details for calculation. A 10 percent further increase in the two levels of minimums in 1967 would have raised the minimum-wage-impact measure more than one and one-half times. For the industry-weighted measure this would be from 0.08 to 0.20 percent. Applying the regression coefficient of $-96.88$ to this 0.12 increment in $MI/W$ yields an estimate of 12 million man-hours lost. This is a 0.7 percent decrease in man-hours for all workers. Since the $MI/W$ measure already is in terms of percentage changes in average wage for all workers and is very small (0.12 percent), this implies a suspiciously large elasticity of $-5.65$. A smaller elasticity, however, is relevant to the workers initially below the minimum. Again using the Labor Department estimates, a 10 percent higher minimum would have directly affected about 7.24 million workers with about 280 million man-hours; and it would have raised their average wage about 4.43 percentage points more than the 9.76 percent increase already required in 1967. So, if all of the additional man-hour loss was within this group (a 4.28 percent loss), it would imply an elasticity of about $-0.97$.[7]

### Effects by Major Industry Division

With the minimum-wage effects almost imperceptible for the total economy, some breakdown of the total into its component parts is

---

[6] In none of the *WAGE*, *NEMP*, or *MANH* equations were the *t*-values significant for the unadjusted form of *MC/W* or the overall form of *MI/W*.

[7] No elasticity was computed here for *MC/W*, which had a coefficient of the wrong sign and was not significant.

needed to reveal more clearly the extent and distribution of its effects. While in most studies this has been done by a breakdown for worker groups, this study focuses on an industry breakdown.

There are eight major industry divisions that sum to the private nonfarm totals in the Labor Department's data series obtained from reports by employing establishments. Coverage ratios for the federal minimums have been estimated by the Employment Standards Administration for each of the eight major industry divisions. Estimates of required payroll increases were made only in total and not for each division, but the 1970 wage-structure survey provides a basis for estimating parameters for all divisions except mining. As a proxy for mining, the parameters of transportation may be used.[8] The two alternative minimum-wage measures for this study, $MC/W$ and $MI/W$, were computed by division before weighting into an average for all private nonfarm industries; so these measures are available for separate industry regressions and are shown in tables 22 and 23, in the appendix.

Identification of the low-wage industries that are expected to be most affected by a minimum-wage rate is a first step of analysis. It might be assumed that a simple rank-ordering of the industries by their average wage would suffice, but this does not indicate an appropriate cutoff point above which the minimum may have had virtually no direct impact. It is the advantage of the new measure of relative minimum-wage impact that it shows where the minimum has no impact at all, that is, where there are no workers below the legal minimum.

Table 3 shows the eight major industry divisions in rank order by average hourly earnings in 1979. For selected years, the peak relative minimum-wage impacts due to raises in minimum-wage rates and in coverage are shown. It is apparent that only three divisions—services, finance,[9] and retail trade (referred to hereafter as retailing)—were ever substantially affected by the minimum. The higher-wage industries never had as much as a 0.2 percent increase in their average wage directly required by the minimum wage, except for manufacturing in 1968 alone. Among the three low-wage industries, services and finance changed rank during the period and ended up with about the same moderate impact of about 0.22 percent. Retailing was the industry most affected by the minimum during every peak year after it became substantially covered in 1961. Accordingly, the

[8] Transportation and public utilities.
[9] Finance, real estate, and insurance.

# TABLE 3

## Relative Minimum-Wage Impact by Major Industry Division, 1950–1979

| Major Industry Division | Average Hourly Earnings 1979 (dollars) | Relative Minimum-Wage Impact (percent) | | | | | | |
|---|---|---|---|---|---|---|---|---|
| | | 1950 | 1956 | 1962 | 1964 | 1968 | 1975 | 1979 |
| Higher wage | | | | | | | | |
| Construction | 9.26 | .15 | .10 | .09 | .10 | .12 | .00 | .02 |
| Mining | 8.48 | .00 | .00 | .00 | .01 | .09 | .00 | .00 |
| Transportation | 8.18 | .18 | .10 | .00 | .00 | .08 | .00 | .00 |
| Manufacturing | 6.69 | .15 | .01 | .01 | .06 | .24 | .00 | .00 |
| Wholesale trade | 6.39 | .05 | .02 | .10 | .00 | .05 | .00 | .00 |
| Lower wage | | | | | | | | |
| Services | 5.36 | .30 | .26 | .15 | .17 | .24 | .02 | .22 |
| Finance | 5.28 | .23 | .20 | .07 | .10 | .43 | .02 | .21 |
| Retail trade | 4.53 | .05 | .05 | .28 | .23 | .52 | .24 | .70 |

Note: See table 23, in the appendix, for data in all years, 1947–1979.
Source: Author.

focus here will be on the minimum-wage effects in these three low-wage industries.

**Wage Effects.** It is well known that wage trends in all industries are very similar. Labor markets appear to be flexible enough to keep average wages rising everywhere with the rising productivity of the economy. The time plots are smooth in each industry, bending upward with accelerating inflation after the mid-1960s. Accordingly, it is possible to use the average wage of the five high-wage industry divisions $(WH)$ as a control variable or predictor of the average wage in each of the three low-wage industries. Examination of each industry's wage plotted on a graph against the high-wage group average shows a very close and smooth linear relation except that there is a slight shift in the line after 1969. The stagflation conditions in the 1970s seem to have caused a somewhat faster rise in wages in the high-wage group after 1969. The equation chosen to reflect wage effects in each low-wage industry, therefore, equates the industry wage as the dependent variable with the alternative minimum-wage measures $(MC/W$ and $MI/W)$ plus the wage of the high-wage group $(WH)$, a zero dummy taking the value of one after 1969 $(D69)$, and a multiple of that dummy and the high-wage average $(WHD)$. The results are shown in table 4.

## TABLE 4

### WAGE EFFECTS IN MAJOR LOW-WAGE INDUSTRY DIVISIONS, 1947–1979

| Dependent | Constant | Minimum-Wage Measures | Other Independent Variables | $R^2$ | Autoregressive (lag) | Correlation |
|---|---|---|---|---|---|---|
| **Services** | | | | | | |
| $WAGE =$ | $-.1315$ | $+ .1836\ MC/W$ (1.2) | $+ .7690\ WH$ (36.1) $\quad + .2931\ D69$ (3.5) $\quad - .0562\ WHD$ (2.5) | .9987 | (3) | .032 |
| $WAGE =$ | $-.1405$ | $- .1154\ MI/W$ (2.2)** | $+ .7921\ WH$ (49.1) $\quad + .2879\ D69$ (3.5) $\quad - .0631\ WHD$ (2.8) | .9986 | (4) | $-.005$ |
| **Finance** | | | | | | |
| $WAGE =$ | $.0786$ | $+ .0936\ MC/W$ (0.9) | $+ .8100\ WH$ (79.0) $\quad + .6281\ D69$ (14.2) $\quad - .1865\ WHD$ (15.3) | .9995 | (2) | $-.008$ |

$$WAGE = .1005 + .0533\ MI/W + .8143\ WH + .6446\ D69 - .1920\ WHD \qquad .9996 \quad (4) \quad .101$$
$$(1.4)^* \qquad (100.5) \qquad (16.8) \qquad (18.7)$$

Retail trade

$$WAGE = .0324 + .2933\ MC/W + .6209\ WH + .1978\ D69 - .0489\ WHD \qquad .9995 \quad (3) \quad -.064$$
$$(4.2)^{***} \qquad (46.6) \qquad (4.4) \qquad (4.0)$$

$$WAGE = -.0282 + .0378\ MI/W + .6603\ WH + .2851\ D69 - .0740\ WHD \qquad .9991 \quad (4) \quad .062$$
$$(1.6)^* \qquad (57.4) \qquad (5.3) \qquad (5.1)$$

NOTES: Symbols for variables: $WAGE$ = average hourly earnings (\$); $MC/W$ = coverage-weighted relative minimum wage (ratio); $MI/W$ = relative minimum-wage impact (percent); $WH$ = average hourly earnings of high-wage group (\$); $D69$ = zero dummy becoming 1 after 1969; $WHD = WH \times D69$. In parentheses are $t$-values, with significance percentages indicated for minimum-wage measures only.

* Significant at 10 percent level.
** Significant at 5 percent level.
*** Significant at 1 percent level.

SOURCES: Bureau of Labor Statistics, *Employment and Earnings, United States, 1909-78,* and monthly issues of *Employment and Earnings.*

45

The regressions are a close fit to the data (the $R^2$ is high) in all three industries, the predominant influence being the wage average of the high-wage group and the break variables also being significant. Both minimum-wage measures clearly show a positive effect on the average wage in retailing, the most affected industry. The conventional measure is highly significant and the new measure only marginally so. In the less affected finance industry, the new measure does better, though only marginally significant, while the conventional measure is not significant. In services the conventional measure is also not significant, while the new measure has the wrong sign.

Table 24, in the appendix, shows the same equation run for each of the five high-wage industries. With a similar close fit to the group wage average and the break variables, in none of these high-wage industries did the minimum-wage measures have a significant effect on the industry average wage. The conclusion must be, therefore, that the legal minimum had a clear effect in raising the industry wage average only in the lowest-wage industry and perhaps marginally so in the next-lowest-wage industry.

An investigation of the effects of pooling the data for the three low-wage industries is shown in table 25, in the appendix. Using annual data, of course, limits the number of observations and makes it more difficult for a regression to show an acceptable level of significance. While some studies have pooled low-wage industries simply by summing the data into group averages, this procedure loses the number of observations available, lets the larger industries dominate, and averages out some of the variation. In this study the variance component technique with the Parks method is used to pool all of the annual observations from the three low-wage industry divisions. A single variable is used for the minimum-wage measure, but the other independent variables have been entered in the regression for each industry separately. In this case, for the wage effects, the conventional minimum-wage measure shows up as having an even more significant positive coefficient for the three industries than for retailing alone. The new minimum-wage measure, however, which had the wrong sign in the services industry, still does not achieve a significant confidence level in the pooled data.

**Employment and Man-Hour Effects.** Employment trends and fluctuations are more diverse among major industry divisions than wages. The pattern for the high-wage group, therefore, does not provide a good predictor of employment in low-wage industries, which seem to have narrower cyclical fluctuations. Using an equation similar to that for the wage effect, one finds some relation of industry employment in the high-wage group but a low overall fit. The minimum-wage measures were not significant and usually had the wrong sign in such an equation. A more general and smoother measure of economy-wide demand seems to be needed as a predictor.

The equation selected to isolate minimum-wage effects on employment and man-hours as the dependent variables, therefore, was one that used the real gross domestic product and the productivity index (for all private nonfarm business) as other independent variables. Again, there seemed to be a break in the mid-1960s in the relations of these overall demand variables to the employment and man-hour measures in the low-wage industries; so two break variables were applied to the productivity variable. This equation consistently showed a very close overall fit.

No clear employment effects, in terms of number of workers, were evident in the three industries' regressions shown in table 5. While the sign was negative for the new minimum-wage measure in all three, it was not significant. For the conventional minimum-wage measure, the sign was wrong in all three.

Clearly adverse man-hour effects for retailing, however, are shown in table 6. Both minimum-wage measures had coefficients with a negative sign at a significance level of 5 percent. Yet in finance neither measure was significant, and in services the conventional measure again had the wrong sign. Of course, the higher-wage industries also showed no evidence of minimum-wage effects. Tables 26 and 27, in the appendix, show that employment and man-hour equations for the other five industries usually have wrong signs or low significance levels in relation to the minimum-wage measures. So it is only in the lowest-wage industry, where the wage effects were clear, that the man-hour effects were clearly adverse.

Stronger evidence of disemployment effects, however, results from pooling the data for the three low-wage industries, as shown in tables 28 and 29, in the appendix. In the employment equation, a significant negative coefficient occurs for the new minimum-wage measure. In the man-hour equations, both measures show significant negative coefficients, the new measure being a little stronger. In this case, no industries had offsetting signs; so the pooled results were reinforcing, and a greater significance of employment and man-hour effects was revealed by the variance component technique.

In any event, the disemployment effects indicated in retailing were substantial. Using 1967 figures as being near the mean values for the whole period, a 10 percent further increase in the minimum-wage rates would have made an addition of 0.5 percentage points to the $MI/W$ measure; the regression coefficient associates this with a

## TABLE 5
### EMPLOYMENT EFFECTS IN MAJOR LOW-WAGE INDUSTRY DIVISIONS, 1947–1979

| Dependent | Constant | Minimum-Wage Measures | Other Independent Variables | $R^2$ | Autoregressive (lag) | Correlation |
|---|---|---|---|---|---|---|
| **Services** | | | | | | |
| $NEMP =$ | 1.358 | $+\ 2.008\ MC/W$ <br> $(1.9)^{**}$ | $+\ .0124\ RGDP\ -\ .2933\ PROD\ -\ 6.469\ D65\ +\ .7030\ PRD$ <br> $(7.0)\quad\quad\ (1.4)\quad\quad\ (3.1)\quad\quad\ (3.0)$ | .9932 | (4) | .073 |
| $NEMP =$ | 1.508 | $-\ .2431\ MI/W$ <br> $(0.5)$ | $+\ .0138\ RGDP\ -\ .3820\ PROD\ -\ 6.879\ D65\ +\ .7524\ PRD$ <br> $(7.8)\quad\quad\ (1.8)\quad\quad\ (3.3)\quad\quad\ (3.3)$ | .9947 | (4) | .033 |
| **Finance** | | | | | | |
| $NEMP =$ | .5193 | $+\ .0023\ MC/W$ <br> $(0.0)$ | $+\ .0029\ RGDP\ -\ .0183\ PROD\ -\ .2287\ D65\ +\ .0162\ PRD$ <br> $(6.7)\quad\quad\ (0.3)\quad\quad\ (0.4)\quad\quad\ (0.2)$ | .9823 | (3) | −.002 |

$$NEMP = .5082 - .0672\ MI/W + .0029\ RGDP - .0169\ PROD - .1684\ D65 + .0095\ PRD \qquad .9837 \quad (4) \quad -.017$$
$$\phantom{NEMP = .5082} (0.7) \phantom{+ .0029\ RG} (6.7) \phantom{DP -} (0.3) \phantom{PROD -} (0.3) \phantom{D65} (0.1)$$

Retail trade

$$NEMP = 5.350 + .4572\ MC/W + .0100\ RGDP - .5066\ PROD - 6.690\ D65 + .7525\ PRD \qquad .9949 \quad (1) \quad .247$$
$$\phantom{NEMP = 5.350} (0.8) \phantom{+ .0100\ RG} (9.5) \phantom{DP -} (4.3) \phantom{PROD -} (5.5) \phantom{D65} (5.6)$$

$$NEMP = 5.266 - .1090\ MI/W + .0107\ RGDP - .5394\ PROD - 6.362\ D65 + .7156\ PRD \qquad .9953 \quad (1) \quad .202$$
$$\phantom{NEMP = 5.266} (0.6) \phantom{+ .0107\ RG} (9.7) \phantom{DP -} (4.3) \phantom{PROD -} (4.9) \phantom{D65} (4.9)$$

NOTES: Symbols for variables: $NEMP$ = number of nonsupervisory workers employed (millions); $MC/W$ = coverage-weighted relative minimum wage (ratio); $MI/W$ = relative minimum-wage impact (percent); $RGDP$ = real gross domestic product, private nonfarm business ($ billions); $PROD$ = productivity index, private nonfarm business; $D65$ = zero dummy becoming 1 after 1965; $PRD = D65 \times PROD$. In parentheses are $t$-values, with significance percentages indicated for minimum-wage measures only.
** Significant at 5 percent level.

SOURCES: Bureau of Labor Statistics, Employment and Earnings, United States, 1909-78, and monthly issues of Employment and Earnings; and Economic Report of the President, January 1980.

## TABLE 6

### MAN-HOUR EFFECTS IN MAJOR LOW-WAGE INDUSTRY DIVISIONS, 1947–1979

| Dependent | Constant | Minimum-Wage Measures | Other Independent Variables | $R^2$ | Auto-regressive (lag) | Correlation |
|---|---|---|---|---|---|---|
| Services | | | | | | |
| $MANH =$ | 64.99 + | 62.14 MC/W <br> (2.0)** | .3665 RGDP − 5.418 PROD − 112.9 D65 + 12.22 PRD <br> (6.9) (0.9) (1.8) (1.7) | .9924 | (4) | .049 |
| $MANH =$ | 68.25 − | 6.457 MI/W <br> (0.4) | .4075 RGDP − 7.815 PROD − 127.9 D65 + 13.97 PRD <br> (7.7) (1.3) (2.0) (2.0) | .9940 | (4) | .000 |

Finance

$MANH = 20.46 - 1.524 \, MC/W + .1041 \, RGDP - .4555 \, PROD + 19.83 \, D65 - .7079 \, PRD$   .9879   (2)   .026
                (0.1)       (7.0)       (0.3)       (0.2)       (0.3)

$MANH = 19.86 - 3.898 \, MI/W + .1033 \, RGDP - .3643 \, PROD + 2.651 \, D65 - .6336 \, PRD$   .9880   (2)   .037
                (1.1)       (7.2)       (0.2)       (0.1)       (0.3)

Retail trade

$MANH = 212.4 - 24.08 \, MC/W + .2301 \, RGDP - 8.057 \, PROD - 147.0 \, D65 + 16.33 \, PRD$   .9968   (4)   .124
                (2.0)**     (9.6)       (3.0)       (5.8)       (5.8)

$MANH = 219.9 - 6.845 \, MI/W + .2341 \, RGDP - 9.957 \, PROD - 130.6 \, D65 + 14.38 \, PRD$   .9969   (4)   .099
                (2.0)**     (9.5)       (3.5)       (4.8)       (4.7)

NOTES: Symbols for variables: $MANH$ = man-hours per week (millions); $MC/W$ = coverage-weighted relative minimum wage (ratio); $MI/W$ = relative minimum-wage impact (percent); $RGDP$ = real gross domestic product, private nonfarm business ($ billions); $PROD$ = productivity index, private nonfarm business; $D65$ = zero dummy becoming 1 after 1965; $PRD = D65 \times PROD$. In parentheses are $t$-values, with significance percentages indicated for minimum-wage measures only.

** Significant at 5 percent level.

SOURCES: Bureau of Labor Statistics, *Employment and Earnings, United States, 1909-78*, and monthly issues of *Employment and Earnings*; and *Economic Report of the President*, January 1980.

3.4 million loss in man-hours. For the 319 million total man-hours in retailing in 1967, this is a −1.073 percent reduction. This indicates an elasticity of −2.15 for all worker man-hours. Since there would be about 30.75 million man-hours below this raised minimum-wage level, the same 3.4 million loss would be 11.13 percent of the man-hours for these workers. Since the 10 percent additional minimum would have raised their wages by 4.34 percentage points, the elasticity for man-hours for below-minimum-wage workers was −2.56.

For the conventional minimum-wage measure, the elasticity would look much smaller. For the same 10 percent higher minimum, the $MC/W$ ratio in 1967 has an increment of 0.0306, which, multiplied by the regression coefficient, shows a decrease of only 0.74 million man-hours. For the 319 million total man-hours in 1967, this is a 0.23 percent reduction; and for a 10 percent wage increase due to the minimum, this is an elasticity of only −0.02 for man-hours for all workers. The same man-hour reduction solely among the 30.75 million man-hours below the minimum wage is a 2.4 percent reduction; for a 10 percent further wage increase due to the minimum, this is an elasticity of only −0.24 for man-hours for below-minimum workers. Not only does the regression predict a much smaller man-hour decrease, but also the percentage increase in wages is assumed to be much larger; so the conventional minimum-wage measure doubly underestimates the elasticity in retailing.

To sum up, the separation of national data into separate major industry divisions has shown clearer evidence on the effects of a minimum wage and how it was distributed. While the overall effects are barely perceptible, the lowest-wage industry, retailing, most clearly shows a strong association of wage increases and man-hour decreases with minimum-wage-rate step increases. The effects in retailing also account for one-third of the overall man-hour losses estimated for the private nonfarm economy. Finally, the demand elasticity for labor in man-hours is well above unity for the new measure, though much below unity for the conventional measure.

# 5
## Effects among Manufacturing Industries

A more intensive study within each major industry division might better reveal the effects of minimum wages, and such a study of the most affected division, retailing, has been undertaken by Belton Fleisher.[1] Unfortunately, a further breakdown of data by detailed subindustry is limited by the length of the time period for which complete and comparable data are available. It is for this reason that most industry studies have focused on manufacturing. This study also will turn to manufacturing in applying its uniform industry break-down approach. There are twenty manufacturing industries with two-digit codes in the Standard Industrial Classification system of the Census Bureau. While manufacturing is a high-wage major industry division, there are low-wage industries within that division.

An initial problem is to identify which manufacturing industries had wages low enough to be affected by the minimums. For this purpose, they may be rank-ordered by their average hourly earnings (excluding overtime) in 1979. Of course, some have shifted in rank from earlier years, and the ranking alone does not indicate at what point the minimum-wage rates began to be effective. So again the relative minimum-wage impact measure is a useful tool for identifying the affected industries. Table 7 shows the relative minimum-wage impacts for selected peak years of each amendment period for manufacturing industries listed in durable and nondurable products groups.

Using this measure, six industries have been selected as low-wage industries affected by minimum-wage rates. They are lumber, furniture, and miscellaneous in the durable products group and textiles, apparel, and leather in the nondurable products group. Two border-line cases were considered as not quite belonging with the high-wage group but were excluded from the low-wage group in this study. The

[1] Belton M. Fleisher, *Minimum Wage Regulation in Retail Trade* (Washington, D.C.: American Enterprise Institute, 1981).

## TABLE 7

### RELATIVE MINIMUM-WAGE IMPACT BY MANUFACTURING INDUSTRY, 1950–1979

| Industry (2-digit) | Average Hourly Earnings 1979 (dollars) | Relative Minimum-Wage Impact (percent) | | | | | | |
|---|---|---|---|---|---|---|---|---|
| | | 1950 | 1956 | 1962 | 1964 | 1968 | 1975 | 1979 |
| Durable goods | | | | | | | | |
| Primary metals | 8.57 | .00 | .00 | .00 | .00 | .00 | .00 | .00 |
| Transportation equipment | 8.11 | .00 | .00 | .00 | .00 | .00 | .00 | .00 |
| Machinery | 6.99 | .00 | .00 | .00 | .00 | .01 | .00 | .00 |
| Fabricated metals | 6.54 | .04 | .02 | .00 | .00 | .11 | .00 | .00 |
| Stone-clay-glass | 6.49 | .16 | .11 | .01 | .01 | .34 | .00 | .00 |
| Electrical equipment | 6.11 | .14 | .11 | .00 | .02 | .31 | .00 | .00 |
| Instruments | 5.98 | .16 | .06 | .00 | .02 | .25 | .00 | .00 |
| Lumber | 5.83 | 1.14 | 1.08 | .67 | .89 | 1.82 | .10 | .05 |
| Furniture | 4.92 | .84 | .72 | .81 | 1.08 | 1.98 | .42 | .84 |
| Miscellaneous | 4.89 | .78 | .81 | .68 | .89 | 1.64 | .42 | .77 |
| Nondurable goods | | | | | | | | |
| Petroleum | 8.92 | .00 | .00 | .00 | .00 | .00 | .00 | .00 |
| Chemicals | 7.29 | .10 | .00 | .00 | .00 | .03 | .03 | .00 |
| Paper | 6.74 | .37 | .24 | .02 | .05 | .31 | .00 | .00 |
| Tobacco | 6.58 | 3.24 | 2.42 | 1.11 | 1.96 | 2.17 | .00 | .00 |
| Food | 5.98 | .54 | .45 | .20 | .31 | .69 | .00 | .01 |
| Rubber | 5.73 | .08 | .02 | .00 | .05 | .42 | .01 | .06 |
| Textiles | 4.47 | 1.06 | 2.65 | 2.88 | 3.72 | 4.41 | 1.44 | .81 |
| Apparel | 4.18 | .71 | 2.39 | 2.38 | 2.93 | 3.78 | 1.99 | 2.83 |
| Leather | 4.14 | 1.62 | 2.20 | 2.16 | 2.72 | 3.87 | 2.03 | 3.20 |

NOTES: Average hourly earnings exclude overtime. Printing, which is not reported for average hourly earnings excluding overtime, is omitted.
SOURCE: U.S. Department of Labor, *Employment and Earnings*, monthly issues.

low-wage industries all had relative minimum-wage impacts exceeding 1 percent in one or more years, and the food industry failed to meet this test. The tobacco industry started with very high impacts, but rapid wage gains dropped it out of this group before the 1974 minimum-wage amendment. Table 30, in the appendix, confirms that the minimums had no significant wage effects in these two marginal industries, although table 31 in the appendix still shows significant employment and man-hour effects for the tobacco industry.

## Some Past Studies

Somewhat different groups of low-wage manufacturing industries have been identified for other studies of minimum wages, and two of these studies are reviewed here. Both used quarterly data, which provide more observations, tending to make it easier to find statistically significant relations.

**The Mixon-Uri Study.** J. Wilson Mixon and Noel D. Uri applied a method of separating trends and trend deviations in employment.[2] This method had been developed by Marvin Kosters and Finis Welch for studying minimum-wage effects among worker groups.[3] The method may be described here in a simplified fashion as separating the quarterly employment level for all manufacturing into a trend component and a deviation-from-trend component. Then two regression equations are run for each industry, determining the industry's share of the overall trend component and its share in the deviation component. A minimum-wage measure, in this case the relative basic minimum ($MB/W$), neglecting coverage since it was close to 100 percent, is introduced into the regressions to see what effect it had on these shares. For the period 1947–1974, the minimum-wage effects were expressed in elasticity measures, as shown in table 32 in the appendix.

In interpreting their results, Mixon and Uri stated that "the cost in terms of lost employment opportunities and cyclical vulnerability of jobs, however, is not easily estimated from the results."[4] This underplays their results because of their focus on the difference between the two elasticities. The earlier Kosters-Welch study had found that the minimum wage reduced the trend shares and increased the deviation shares of youth and nonwhites. Kosters and Welch called the difference in the elasticity coefficients a "coefficient of

[2] J. Wilson Mixon and Noel D. Uri, "The Effects of Minimum Wages on the Distribution of Changes in Aggregate Employment among Manufacturing Industries," *Review of Business and Economic Research*, vol. 13, no 2 (Winter 1977–78), pp. 56–70.
[3] Marvin Kosters and Finis Welch, "The Effects of Minimum Wages on the Distribution of Changes in Aggregate Employment," *American Economic Review*, vol. 62, no. 3 (June 1972), pp. 323–32.
[4] Mixon and Uri, "Effects of Minimum Wages."

marginality";[5] their results showed increased cyclical vulnerability for the already disadvantaged groups. Mixon and Uri were impressed that their results did not have a positive difference in the coefficients, showing a similar increased vulnerability for low-wage industries. Their study did show, however, that the minimum-wage coefficients were negative in sign for employment effects, both for the trend component and for the deviation component, for six of the seven low-wage industries. The exception was for the apparel industry. This means that the minimum decreased the industry share of over-all employment in both components, which sum together for a total employment effect, although few of the coefficients were significant.

**The Zucker Study.** Albert Zucker did a study of minimum-wage effects on the wage, employment, and man-hours in a group of low-wage industries, using quarterly data for the 1947–1966 period.[6] His low-wage industries were mostly at the three-digit level of industry classification in the nondurables categories of food, textiles, apparel, and leather, although he included one two-digit industry, tobacco, and two four-digit fertilizer categories within the chemicals group. His data were summed for the group as a whole. Then, deducting the group totals from that for all manufacturing, he introduced the residuals for a high-wage group into his regressions as a control variable. For the minimum-wage measure, he used the relative basic minimum wage with the wage deflator lagged one period (which tends to reduce the feedback effect of the wage on the minimum-wage measure). A time variable and a lagged dependent variable were additional independent variables in his equation.

Zucker's regressions, as shown in table 33 in the appendix, all had the expected signs for the minimum-wage coefficients with significance levels of 5 percent or lower. This means that the minimum clearly increased the wage and reduced employment and man-hours. The study period for these results, however, ended before the 1967 amendment, and the results were not shown for individual industries.

### Effects with the New Minimum-Wage Measure

**Wage Effects.** This study extends the comparison of the conventional and new minimum-wage measures to the six most affected low-wage

[5] Kosters and Welch, "Effects of Minimum Wages."

[6] Albert Zucker, "Minimum Wages and the Long-Run Elasticity of Demand for Low-Wage Labor," *Quarterly Journal of Economics*, vol. 87, no. 2 (May 1973), pp. 266–77.

manufacturing industries at the two-digit level of classification. A procedure similar to Zucker's was used, and a wage average for the remaining high-wage industries was computed as a control variable. Separate averages were computed for the durables group and the nondurables group (excluding the food and tobacco industries). Again, since a break in the relations was apparent for the stagflation decade of the 1970s, a zero dummy that becomes one after 1969 was introduced and with it a multiple of the dummy and the control wage. Together with the alternative minimum-wage measures, these were used as independent variables in an equation determining the wage for each industry, as shown in table 8.

For the new minimum-wage measure $(MI/W)$, the coefficients had the expected positive sign for five of the six industries, and in four of these the coefficient was significant. The furniture industry did not show an increase in average wage, and textiles did not show a significant increase. For the conventional minimum, however, positive signs occurred in only four industries, and none was significant. The overall fit of all equations was high, the other variables were all significant, and the predominant influence was the control variable.

Again for these wage equations, a pooling of the three durables industries and of the three nondurables industries did not help. As shown in table 34, in the appendix, none of the signs for the minimum coefficient was significant, and the wrong sign occurred for the conventional minimum-wage measure in the nondurables industry group. This may be because industries within each group had differing signs for the two break dummies. The smooth time trend for wages in all industries seems to make it difficult to discern the minimum-wage impacts.

**Employment and Man-Hour Effects.** Again, as in the case of industry divisions, the manufacturing industries have more diverse trends and fluctuations in employment than in wages. Zucker's study suggests, however, that among manufacturing industries the high-wage group averages could serve as control variables or predictors for each low-wage industry, and a separation of durables and nondurables industry groups might help. Examination of the relations among industries suggested that at least two breaks occurred, in 1951 and 1961 for the durables group and in 1961 and 1969 for the nondurables group. Accordingly, both the employment and man-hour equations included the alternative minimum-wage measure, a high-wage control group average, and two pairs of dummy variables, as shown in table 9 and table 10.

## TABLE 8
### WAGE EFFECTS IN LOW-WAGE MANUFACTURING INDUSTRIES, 1947–1979

| Dependent | Constant | Minimum-Wage Measures | Other Independent Variables | | | $R^2$ | Autoregressive (lag) | Correlation |
|---|---|---|---|---|---|---|---|---|
| *Durables industries* | | | | | | | | |
| **Lumber** | | | | | | | | |
| $WAGE$ = | .1376 | + .0412 MC/W (0.5) | + .7062 WH (33.6) | − .4027 D69 (3.9) | + .1458 WD (5.1) | .9981 | (3) | .114 |
| $WAGE$ = | .1707 | + .0219 MI/W (1.4)* | + .6965 WH (36.4) | − .4165 D69 (4.6) | + .1555 WD (6.1) | .9985 | (3) | .034 |
| **Furniture** | | | | | | | | |
| $WAGE$ = | .2491 | − .0656 MC/W (0.8) | + .6718 WH (37.3) | + .3000 D69 (3.6) | − .0620 WD (2.7) | .9978 | (4) | −.048 |
| $WAGE$ = | .2227 | − .0121 MI/W (0.9) | + .6702 WH (40.3) | + .3856 D69 (3.8) | − .0588 WD (2.8) | .9982 | (4) | −.065 |
| **Miscellaneous** | | | | | | | | |
| $WAGE$ = | .1991 | − .0063 MC/W (0.1) | + .6824 WH (51.3) | + .3796 D69 (5.7) | − .0803 WD (4.4) | .9985 | (3) | −.010 |
| $WAGE$ = | .2057 | + .0154 MI/W (1.3)* | + .6747 WH (52.7) | + .3820 D69 (6.2) | − .0762 WD (4.5) | .9989 | (3) | −.011 |

*Nondurables industries*

Textiles

$WAGE = .4751 + .1648\ MC/W + .4146\ WH - .5301\ D64 + .2410\ WD$    .9983    (1)    .002
$\qquad\qquad\quad\ (1.1)\qquad\quad (10.1)\qquad (4.8)\qquad\ (5.5)$

$WAGE = .5263 + .0086\ MI/W + .4325\ WH - .4920\ D64 + .2245\ WD$    .9982    (1)    .005
$\qquad\qquad\quad\ (0.8)\qquad\quad (12.1)\qquad (4.6)\qquad\ (5.5)$

Apparel

$WAGE = .5319 + .0511\ MC/W + .4315\ WH - .1440\ D66 + .1065\ WD$    .9980    (1)    .027
$\qquad\qquad\quad\ (0.4)\qquad\quad (13.4)\qquad (1.6)\qquad\ (3.2)$

$WAGE = .6102 + .0276\ MI/W + .3935\ WH - .2478\ D66 + .1448\ WD$    .9987    (4)    −.001
$\qquad\qquad\quad (3.0)**\qquad (17.3)\qquad (3.6)\qquad\ (5.9)$

Leather

$WAGE = .2002 + .0577\ MC/W + .5875\ WH + .3463\ D69 + .0767\ WD$    .9955    (2)    .026
$\qquad\qquad\quad\ (0.4)\qquad\quad (18.6)\qquad (3.1)\qquad\ (2.7)$

$WAGE = .2619 + .0243\ MI/W + .5612\ WH + .3340\ D69 + .0617\ WD$    .9956    (2)    .045
$\qquad\qquad\quad (1.7)*\qquad\ (19.0)\qquad (3.2)\qquad\ (2.0)$

NOTES: Symbols for variables: $WAGE$ = average hourly earnings ($); $MC/W$ = relative minimum wage (ratio); $MI/W$ = relative minimum-wage impact (percent); $WH$ = average hourly earnings of high-wage group, durables or nondurables manufacturing ($); $D64$, $D66$, $D69$ = zero dummy becoming 1 after 1964, 1966, 1969, respectively; $WD = D \times WH$ (for indicated year). In parentheses are $t$-values, with significance percentages indicated for minimum-wage measures only.

* Significant at 10 percent level.

** Significant at 5 percent level.

SOURCES: U.S. Department of Labor, Bureau of Labor Statistics, *Employment and Earnings, United States, 1909-78,* bulletin 1312-11, and monthly issues of *Employment and Earnings.*

## TABLE 9
### EMPLOYMENT EFFECTS IN LOW-WAGE MANUFACTURING INDUSTRIES, 1947–1979

| Dependent | Constant | Minimum-Wage Measures | Other Independent Variables | | | | | | $R^2$ | (lag) | Autoregressive Correlation |
|---|---|---|---|---|---|---|---|---|---|---|---|

*Durables industries*

**Lumber**

$NEMP = .2810 - .1571\ MC/W + .1036\ NH - .3245\ D51 + .0254\ ND1 + .1142\ D61 - .0629\ ND2$
  (1.9)** (2.6) (1.2) (0.5) (0.5) (1.4)  
  $R^2 = .8710$ (1) −.035

$NEMP = .2998 - .0272\ MI/W + .0884\ NH - .4641\ D51 + .0477\ ND1 - .0030\ D61 - .0443\ ND2$
  (2.3)** (2.4) (1.8) (1.0) (0.0) (1.1)  
  $R^2 = .8856$ (1) −.087

**Furniture**

$NEMP = .1600 + .0315\ MC/W - .0202\ NH - .0075\ D51 + .0006\ ND1 - .1752\ D61 - .0330\ ND2$
  (0.6) (1.4) (0.1) (0.0) (1.8) (2.0)  
  $R^2 = .8873$ (3) −.066

$NEMP = .1573 - .0101\ MI/W + .0239\ NH + .0638\ D51 - .0113\ ND1 - .1406\ D61 - .0286\ ND2$
  (1.5)* (1.6) (0.6) (0.6) (1.5) (1.7)  
  $R^2 = .9064$ (2) −.013

**Miscellaneous**

$NEMP = .2136 - .0652\ MC/W + .0305\ NH - .0564\ D51 + .0025\ ND1 + .0137\ D61 - .0092\ ND2$
  (2.6)*** (2.8) (0.8) (0.2) (0.2) (0.8)  
  $R^2 = .8319$ (2) .025

$NEMP = .2346 - .0073\ MI/W + .0215\ NH - .1159\ D51 + .0123\ ND1 - .0489\ D61 + .0010\ ND2$
  (1.6)* (2.0) (1.6) (0.9) (0.8) (0.1)  
  $R^2 = .7951$ (2) .011

*Nondurables industries*

**Textiles**

$$NEMP = 2.882 - \underset{(1.9)**}{.4171} MC/W - \underset{(2.8)}{.8567} NH - \underset{(3.2)}{2.261} D61 + \underset{(3.2)}{1.093} ND1 - \underset{(2.3)}{1.795} D69 + \underset{(2.3)}{.8585} ND2 \quad .7978 \quad (4) \quad -.029$$

$$NEMP = 3.104 - \underset{(1.7)**}{.0340} MI/W - \underset{(4.4)}{1.082} NH - \underset{(4.4)}{2.711} D61 + \underset{(4.5)}{1.331} ND1 - \underset{(2.8)}{2.103} D69 + \underset{(3.0)}{1.025} ND2 \quad .8018 \quad (1) \quad -.002$$

**Apparel**

$$NEMP = .4969 - \underset{(1.2)}{.1364} MC/W + \underset{(2.0)}{.3447} NH + \underset{(0.5)}{.1880} D61 - \underset{(0.4)}{.0695} ND1 + \underset{(0.9)}{.4106} D69 - \underset{(1.0)}{.2027} ND2 \quad .6875 \quad (3) \quad -.027$$

$$NEMP = .4981 - \underset{(3.0)***}{.0305} MI/W + \underset{(2.8)}{.3167} NH + \underset{(0.1)}{.0323} D61 + \underset{(0.2)}{.0232} ND1 - \underset{(1.2)}{.3713} D69 - \underset{(1.2)}{.1742} ND2 \quad .8020 \quad (2) \quad .023$$

**Leather**

$$NEMP = .4338 - \underset{(2.4)***}{.1030} MC/W - \underset{(0.3)}{.0174} NH - \underset{(0.3)}{.0392} D61 - \underset{(0.4)}{.0246} ND1 - \underset{(0.0)}{.0066} D69 - \underset{(0.5)}{.0326} ND2 \quad .9122 \quad (4) \quad -.053$$

$$NEMP = .4902 - \underset{(2.8)***}{.0097} MI/W - \underset{(1.6)}{.0737} NH - \underset{(1.0)}{.1106} D61 + \underset{(0.9)}{.0522} ND1 - \underset{(1.1)}{.1374} D69 + \underset{(0.6)}{.0330} ND2 \quad .9224 \quad (3) \quad .028$$

NOTES: Symbols for variables: $NEMP$ = number of nonsupervisory workers employed (millions); $MC/W$ = relative minimum wage (ratio); $MI/W$ = relative minimum-wage impact (percent); $NH$ = number employed in high-wage group, durables or nondurables manufacturing (millions); $D51$, $D61$, $D69$ = zero dummy becoming 1 after 1951, 1961, 1969, respectively; $ND1$ and $ND2 = D \times NH$ (for indicated year). In parentheses are $t$-values, with significance percentages indicated for minimum-wage measures only.

\* Significant at 10 percent level.   \*\* Significant at 5 percent level.   \*\*\* Significant at 1 percent level.

SOURCES: Bureau of Labor Statistics, *Employment and Earnings, United States, 1909–78*, and monthly issues of *Employment and Earnings*.

## TABLE 10
### MAN-HOUR EFFECTS IN LOW-WAGE MANUFACTURING INDUSTRIES, 1947–1979

| Dependent | Constant | Minimum-Wage Measures | Other Independent Variables | $R^2$ | Autoregressive (lag) | Correlation |
|---|---|---|---|---|---|---|
| *Durables industries* | | | | | | |
| **Lumber** | | | | | | |
| $MANH =$ | 14.99 − | 6.857 MC/W + (2.0)** | .8480 MH − 12.31 D51 + .2275 MD1 + 2.514 D61 − .4961 MD2 | .8521 | (1) | −.010 |
| | | (2.6) | (1.3) (0.6) (0.3) (1.4) | | | |
| $MANH =$ | 15.91 − | 1.212 MI/W + (2.6)*** | .6809 MH − 18.35 D51 + .4639 MD1 − 2.786 D61 − .2901 MD2 | .8912 | (2) | −.087 |
| | | (2.2) | (2.1) (1.2) (0.4) (0.9) | | | |
| **Furniture** | | | | | | |
| $MANH =$ | 6.506 + | .7212 MC/W + (0.3) | .2187 MH + .2480 D51 − .0251 MD1 − 5.924 D61 + .2674 MD2 | .8617 | (2) | .063 |
| | | (1.5) | (0.1) (0.1) (1.5) (1.6) | | | |
| $MANH =$ | 6.147 − | .3472 MI/W + (1.2) | .2544 MH + 2.074 D51 − .1012 MD1 − 4.873 D61 + .2323 MD2 | .8932 | (2) | −.003 |
| | | (1.9) | (0.5) (0.6) (1.4) (1.6) | | | |
| **Miscellaneous** | | | | | | |
| $MANH =$ | 9.386 − | 1.060 MC/W + (0.9) | .2380 MH − 4.870 D51 + .1189 MD1 − 1.231 D61 − .0394 MD2 | .8417 | (4) | .035 |
| | | (2.6) | (2.0) (1.1) (0.5) (0.4) | | | |
| $MANH =$ | 9.706 + | .0127 MI/W + (0.1) | 2.026 MH − 5.915 D51 + .1592 MD1 − 2.161 D61 − .0047 MD2 | .8568 | (4) | .003 |
| | | (2.5) | (2.7) (1.7) (1.0) (0.1) | | | |

*Nondurables industries*

**Textiles**

$$MANH = 75.95 - 24.16 \; MC/W - .0287 \; MH - 43.86 \; D61 + .0508 \; MD1 - 32.19 \; D69 + .0338 \; MD2 \quad .6781 \; (4) \quad .006$$
$$(3.1)^{***} \qquad\qquad (1.6) \qquad\qquad (2.0) \qquad\qquad (1.3) \qquad\qquad (1.3)$$

$$MANH = 77.17 - 2.220 \; MI/W - .0453 \; MH - 59.13 \; D61 + .0710 \; MD1 - 36.20 \; D69 + .0401 \; MD2 \quad .6824 \; (1) \quad .017$$
$$(2.7)^{***} \qquad\qquad (2.6) \qquad\qquad (2.7) \qquad\qquad (2.8) \qquad\qquad (1.4) \qquad\qquad (1.4)$$

**Apparel**

$$MANH = 29.05 - 2.733 \; MC/W + .0141 \; MH - 5.045 \; D61 + .0093 \; MD1 - .5450 \; D69 + .0007 \; MD2 \quad .6542 \; (2) \quad .088$$
$$(0.7) \qquad\qquad (1.6) \qquad\qquad (0.5) \qquad\qquad (0.7) \qquad\qquad (0.0) \qquad\qquad (0.1)$$

$$MANH = 26.53 - 1.035 \; MI/W + .0164 \; MH - 6.504 \; D61 + .0124 \; MD1 + 3.986 \; D69 - .0036 \; MD2 \quad .7875 \; (1) \quad .028$$
$$(2.7)^{***} \qquad\qquad (2.3) \qquad\qquad (0.7) \qquad\qquad (1.2) \qquad\qquad (0.4) \qquad\qquad (0.3)$$

**Leather**

$$MANH = 159.0 - 44.67 \; MC/W - .0069 \; MH + 6.270 \; D61 - 0.117 \; MD1 + 8.740 \; D69 - .0432 \; MD2 \quad .8952 \; (3) \quad .009$$
$$(2.6)^{***} \qquad\qquad (0.2) \qquad\qquad (0.1) \qquad\qquad (0.2) \qquad\qquad (0.2) \qquad\qquad (0.8)$$

$$MANH = 163.0 - 4.849 \; MI/W - .0396 \; MH - 36.21 \; D61 + .0422 \; MD1 - 31.52 \; D69 + .0047 \; MD2 \quad .9180 \; (4) \quad -.007$$
$$(3.3)^{***} \qquad\qquad (1.3) \qquad\qquad (0.9) \qquad\qquad (0.9) \qquad\qquad (0.7) \qquad\qquad (0.1)$$

NOTES: Symbols for variables: $MANH$ = man-hours per week (millions); $MC/W$ = relative minimum wage (ratio); $MI/W$ = relative minimum-wage impact (percent); $MH$ = man-hours in high-wage group, durables or nondurables manufacturing (millions); $D51$, $D61$, $D69$ = zero dummy becoming 1 after 1951, 1961, 1969, respectively; $MD1$ and $MD2 = D \times MH$ (for indicated year). In parentheses are $t$-values, with significance percentages indicated for minimum-wage measures only.

** Significant at 5 percent level.

*** Significant at 1 percent level.

SOURCES: Bureau of Labor Statistics, *Employment and Earnings, United States, 1908–78*, and monthly issues of *Employment and Earnings*.

In terms of number of workers, the disemployment effects were clearly evident in the negative signs for the minimum-wage measures in all employment equations but one. For the new measure all coefficients were significant, and for the conventional minimum-wage measure, all but two. The overall fit of the equation was high, and the coefficient of the control variable was significant, but many of the break dummies were not individually significant in this uniform approach.

In terms of man-hours, the negative effects were not as clear in all of these industries. For the new measure, the coefficient was not significant in the furniture industry and had the wrong sign in the miscellaneous category. For the conventional measure, the coefficient was not significant or had the wrong sign in three industries. The overall fit also was a little less in the man-hour equations.

In this case, the pooling technique seems to work, as shown in tables 35 and 36, in the appendix. For the pooled durables industries, both minimum-wage measures had significantly negative signs for both employment and man-hour equations. The significance was weaker for man-hours, but in both equations it was stronger than might be expected from the individual industries. For the pooled nondurables industries, both measures had negative signs in both equations, although for the employment equation the coefficient was of marginal significance for the new minimum-wage measure and was not significant for the conventional measure. For the man-hour equation, both had strongly significant negative coefficients, and more so than might have been expected from the individual industry equations.

The magnitude of these disemployment effects for the lowest-wage manufacturing industry, leather, is comparable to those in retailing in relative terms, though not in absolute numbers. Using actual data for 1966, which are close to the mean values of the regressions, one finds that a 10 percent further increase in the minimum-wage rate would have increased the required payroll increase by 1.215 percentage points. Multiplied by the coefficient in the man-hours equation, this implies a reduction of 5.89 million man-hours, or a decrease of 4.79 percent; so the elasticity is —3.94 for all workers. The additional 10 percent in the minimum wage would have brought 27.4 million workers below the minimum; but, since many of them were well above the existing minimum, an additional increase of only 4.6 percentage points in their average wage would have been required. The same loss of man-hours for only this group of workers would be a 21.52 percent loss; so the elasticity for below-minimum workers is —4.68.

For the conventional minimum-wage measure, the elasticity would look much smaller. A 10 percent higher minimum wage would raise the 1966 $MC/W$ ratio by 0.0673 points, which, multiplied by the regression coefficient, implies a reduction of 3.00 million man-hours. For the 122.9 million total worker man-hours in 1966, this is a loss of 2.446 percent, which, with the 10 percent increase in wage due to the raised minimums, implies an elasticity of only $-0.24$ for all worker man-hours. The same loss within the 27.37 million man-hours below the minimum implies a 10.98 percent reduction, which, with the 10 percent increase in wage due to the raised minimum, implies an elasticity of $-1.10$. This is greater than unity but still lower than for the new minimum-wage measure because the regression estimates a smaller man-hour loss and the assumed wage increase. is much larger.

The industry breakdown approach, therefore, shows significant and substantial disemployment effects for the lowest-wage industries within the high-wage manufacturing division. The elasticities again are larger for the new minimum-wage measure, but even the conventional measure shows an elasticity greater than unity for man-hours of below-minimum workers. More intensive study might develop closer-fitting equations for each industry, and a finer breakdown of industry classifications might show even greater minimum-wage effects. But these were beyond the scope of this study.

### Effects among Regions

It would seem that regional breakdowns would provide another useful approach to studying minimum-wage effects. It is well known, for example, that the South has lower wage averages, and uniform national minimum-wage rates would be expected to have a greater effect on this region. Account must first be taken, however, of the industry mix by region, for there is a heavier concentration of low-wage industries in the South. Even studies of the same industry in different regions must be approached with caution, for the other independent variables may differ by region. In retailing, for example, the market is quite local; so the demand for workers depends on incomes, population trends, and other conditions peculiar to a region.

A regional breakdown within low-wage manufacturing industries avoids some of this difficulty, because the competitive market is presumed to be more national in scope. To a considerable extent the competitive effects between high-wage and low-wage employers are reflected in regional competition. This approach still must be taken with caution because there remain industry-mix and product-mix differences within broad industry classifications. Many manufacturing industries are concentrated near resources or near regional population centers. It becomes more of an empirical question than a theoretical prediction of how minimum-wage effects will be distributed regionally. It is a question, however, that has long been of widespread interest.

**The Nussbaum-Wise Study.** Joyce M. Nussbaum and Donald E. Wise have made a key study of the regional effects of minimum wages within manufacturing.[7] Selecting five low-wage industries for study—textiles, apparel, leather, lumber, and furniture—they were able to construct complete totals for the South in each industry by using the state data available in the *Census of Manufactures* and the *Annual Survey of Manufactures* (supplemented by data from *County Business Patterns* for some data allocations in the leather industry).[8] Deducting the figures on the South from national totals gave them residuals for the "North." For each region they summed the five industries into one group, and their data were on an annual basis for the period 1951–1973. Since their source provided average hourly earnings, average weekly hours, and number of production workers, they could run separate regressions for wage, employment, and man-hours as dependent variables. For a minimum-wage measure, they followed Zucker in using the relative basic minimum with the wage deflator lagged one year to reduce the feedback effect; however, they subtracted this ratio from one so that the expected sign of the coefficients would be reversed. They also used a control variable for a high-wage group of manufacturing industries plus time and time squared as their other independent variables. They also ran separate regressions for the control group using real gross national product as the demand variable.

What Nussbaum and Wise achieved with their data construction was a four-way division of all manufacturing. They had a low-wage industry group and a high-wage industry group; and for each they had a South group and a North group. What they first did with this breakdown was to treat it as two successive two-way comparisons, as shown in table 37, in the appendix. For all manufacturing in the

---

[7] Joyce M. Nussbaum and Donald E. Wise, "The Impact of the Federal Minimum Wage on the Geographic Distribution of Employment," prepared by Mathtech, Inc., Princeton, New Jersey, for the U.S. Department of Labor, February 1977 (processed, National Technical Information Service, no. PB 266070).

[8] The *Census of Manufactures* and the *Annual Survey of Manufactures* are available from the U.S. Department of Commerce. *County Business Patterns* is available from the U.S. Department of Labor.

North, the minimum-wage measure had no significant effect either on average wage or on employment and man-hours. For all manufacturing in the South, there was a significant effect on wage but not on employment or man-hours. For all high-wage industries nationally (both regions combined), the minimum-wage measure had no significant effect on the average wage or on employment and man-hours. But for low-wage industries nationally, the minimum-wage measure had a significant effect in raising the average wage and in reducing employment and man-hours. These results are consistent with the analysis in this study of the all-manufacturing division and of the low-wage industries within manufacturing.

Nussbaum and Wise then did a four-way analysis with their data breakdown of manufacturing. They ran separate regressions for high-wage and low-wage industries within the North and within the South, as shown in table 11. It should be remembered that the reverse signs in this table are expected for this minimum-wage measure. Starting with the high-wage North, using real GNP and a lagged dependent variable plus time as predictors, they found no significant effect of the minimum-wage measure. For the low-wage North, however, the minimum had a significant effect in raising the average wage and lowering employment and man-hours.

For the South almost the same result occurred. For the high-wage industries in the South, the minimum wage did have a significant effect in raising the average wage, but there was no significant effect on employment and man-hours. But for the low-wage industries in the South, the minimum wage had a significant effect both in raising the average wage and in lowering employment and man-hours.

Thus, empirically there is little evidence that the minimum-wage effects fall more heavily on the South within manufacturing industries. The burden clearly is greater on low-wage industries wherever they exist. While they are concentrated a little more in the South, the effects do not show up more clearly for all manufacturing or within low-wage manufacturing industries in the South, at least not in time series data.

**Long-Term Effects by Region.** This study should not end without this note of caution about the time series data. Aside from the difficulty in distinguishing any trends in minimum-wage effect from other independent trends, there also is a difficulty in distinguishing long-term adjustments. The time series regressions are useful in determining whether the saw-toothed step increases in minimum rates are noticeably associated with accelerated wage increases or diminished employment and man-hour changes. The statistical tool is limited in

## TABLE 11
### MINIMUM-WAGE EFFECTS ON MANUFACTURING, BY WAGE LEVEL AND BY REGION, 1951–1973

| Dependent | Constant | Minimum-Wage Measure | Other Independent Variables | | | | $R^2$ | DW |
|---|---|---|---|---|---|---|---|---|
| **North, high-wage (nh)** | | | | | | | | |
| $\ln W_{nh} =$ | 1.52 | $- .031 M_{nh}$ <br> (0.5) | $- .07 \ln G$ <br> (0.7) | $- .015 T$ <br> (1.3) | $+ .0018 T^2$ <br> (5.4) | | .998 | 1.55 |
| $\ln E_{nh} =$ | −7.80 | $+ .028 M_{nh}$ <br> (0.3) | $+ 1.62 \ln G$ <br> (9.0) | $- .047 T$ <br> (9.1) | $- .0004 T^2$ <br> (2.7) | $+ .32 \ln E_{nh-1}$ <br> (3.9) | .901 | 2.19 |
| $\ln MH_{nh} =$ | −8.22 | $+ .012 M_{nh}$ <br> (0.1) | $+ 1.95 \ln G$ <br> (12.3) | $- .056 T$ <br> (12.0) | $- .0005 T^2$ <br> (4.2) | $+ .17 \ln MH_{nh-1}$ <br> (2.4) | .941 | 2.16 |
| **North, low-wage (nl)** | | | | | | | | |
| $\ln W_{nl} =$ | .02 | $- .105 M_{nl}$ <br> (3.4)*** | $+ .54 \ln W_{nh}$ <br> (5.7) | $- .012 T$ <br> (3.1) | $+ .0010 T^2$ <br> (13.1) | | .998 | 1.70 |
| $\ln E_{nl} =$ | 1.84 | $+ .111 M_{nl}$ <br> (1.9)** | $+ .53 \ln E_{nh}$ <br> (5.8) | $+ .019 T$ <br> (4.5) | $+ .0002 T^2$ <br> (1.3) | | .961 | 2.03 |
| $\ln MH_{nl} =$ | 1.30 | $+ .078 M_{nl}$ <br> (1.5)* | $+ .59 \ln MH_{nh}$ <br> (7.8) | $+ .018 T$ <br> (4.7) | $+ .0001 T^2$ <br> (1.1) | | .969 | 1.77 |

South, high-wage (sh)

$$\ln W_{sh} = -.25 + .088\, M_{sh} + 1.14\ln W_{nh} - .006\, T + .0001\, T^2 \qquad\qquad\qquad\qquad .999 \quad 2.44$$
$$\phantom{\ln W_{sh} = -.25 +\ } (3.1)^{***} \quad (10.1) \qquad (1.6) \qquad (0.5)$$

$$\ln E_{sh} = -1.68 + .021\, M_{sh} + .56\ln E_{nh} + .014\, T + .0002\, T^2 + .27\ln E_{sh-1} \qquad .997 \quad 2.05$$
$$\phantom{\ln E_{sh} = -1.68 +\ } (0.5) \qquad (9.1) \qquad (5.3) \qquad (3.3) \qquad (3.8)$$

$$\ln MH_{sh} = -1.80 + .008\, M_{sh} + .59\ln MH_{nh} + .015\, T + .0002\, T^2 + .26\ln MH_{sh-1} \quad .997 \quad 1.80$$
$$\phantom{\ln MH_{sh} = -1.80 +\ } (0.2) \qquad (11.0) \qquad (6.5) \qquad (2.6) \qquad (4.0)$$

South, low-wage (sl)

$$\ln W_{sl} = -.25 + .064\, M_{sl} + .56\ln W_{nh} - .014\, T + .0012\, T^2 \qquad\qquad\qquad\qquad .999 \quad 2.22$$
$$\phantom{\ln W_{sl} = -.25 +\ } (4.4)^{***} \quad (6.9) \qquad (4.3) \qquad (17.3)$$

$$\ln E_{sl} = .80 + .020\, M_{sl} + .56\ln E_{nh} - .006\, T + .0007\, T^2 \qquad\qquad\qquad\qquad .985 \quad 1.88$$
$$\phantom{\ln E_{sl} = .80 +\ } (0.8) \qquad (7.9) \qquad (1.2) \qquad (4.3)$$

$$\ln MH_{sl} = -.29 + .052\, M_{sl} + .67\ln MH_{nh} + .007\, T + .0003\, T^2 \qquad\qquad\qquad .976 \quad 1.94$$
$$\phantom{\ln MH_{sl} = -.29 +\ } (1.5)^{*} \quad (7.9) \qquad (1.2) \qquad (1.7)$$

NOTES: Low-wage industries include textiles, apparel, lumber, furniture, leather. High-wage industries include all other manufacturing. Symbols for variables: $W$ = average hourly earnings (\$); $M = (1 - M/W_{-1})$, 1 minus the relative minimum wage with a lagged wage deflator; $E$ = employed workers (thousands); $MH$ = man-hours per week (millions); $G$ = real gross national product; $T$ = year minus 1946. The ln indicates a log of the variable. $DW$ = Durbin-Watson statistic. In parentheses are $t$-values, with significance levels indicated for minimum-wage measures only. Note that the subtraction of the relative minimum wage reverses all expected signs on the coefficients.

\* Significant at 10 percent level.

\*\* Significant at 5 percent level.

\*\*\* Significant at 1 percent level.

SOURCE: Nussbaum and Wise, "Impact of the Federal Minimum Wage."

this regard. While the time series effects have been observed only for short periods, say within the initial quarter or year after a rate increase, some of the adjustments may take longer. Capital adjustments in terms of labor-saving equipment or of plant relocations may take place gradually and over longer periods. In addition, once employers have observed repeated legislative amendments raising the rates, they may anticipate future increases in the minimum. This reinforces their plans to make long-term adjustments and may even lead to short-term adjustments in advance of the date of rate increases.

A key study of long-term effects by region was made by David E. Kaun in one of the earliest minimum-wage studies.[9] He used *Census of Manufactures* data for 1939, 1947, and 1958 to compare employment changes by region in twenty low-wage manufacturing industries. The results are summarized in table 12. While the employment growth rate in all manufacturing was comparable in the South and the non-South from 1939 to 1947, from 1947 to 1958 the non-South experienced a decline while the South continued to expand. In terms of industry group totals, the low-wage industries were declining in the non-South before and after 1947, while in the South they expanded before 1947 but declined to 1958—which was after both the 1950 and the 1956 minimum-wage rate increases. The share of all-manufacturing employment in the low-wage group declined in both regions in both periods, but this decline in share slowed in the non-South and accelerated in the South under the minimums.

Kaun also expressed this experience as correlations of the changes among the twenty industries. In each region, the preminimum percentage changes in employment had about a 0.6 correlation with the postminimum percentage changes at a 5 percent significance level. The preminimum low-wage share of all manufacturing jobs also correlated well with the postminimum share, though not as well in the South. Using the non-South as a control group to predict the South in the preminimum period, there also was a correlation of about 0.6 between percentage changes in the non-South and percentage changes in the South among the twenty industries. In the postminimum period, however, the non-South employment changes were no longer a good predictor of the employment changes in the South in the same low-wage industries. The correlations fell and lost significance.

While a lot of independent changes may influence such long-term comparisons, Kaun's study does suggest that the minimum wages may

[9] David E. Kaun, "Economics of the Minimum Wage: The Effects of the Fair Labor Standards Act, 1945–60" (Ph.D. diss., Stanford University, 1963).

## TABLE 12
### Long-Term Changes in Low-Wage Manufacturing, by Region, 1939–1947 and 1947–1958

| Industry Group and Region | Data in Number of Workers | | Data in Share of Total | |
|---|---|---|---|---|
| *Comparison of percent changes by group* | | | | |
| | (percent change) | | (percentage point change) | |
| | 1939–47 | 1947–58 | 1939–47 | 1947–58 |
| All manufacturing | | | | |
| Non-South | 53 | − 7 | — | — |
| South | 48 | 15 | — | — |
| Low-wage industries | | | | |
| Non-South | −15 | −18 | −45 | −12 |
| South | 31 | − 4 | −11 | −16 |
| *Correlations among twenty industries* | | | | |
| *Preminimum Change to Postminimum Change* | | | | |
| Low-wage industries | | | | |
| Non-South | | .64** | | .73*** |
| South | | .60** | | .44** |
| *Non-South Change to South Change* | | | | |
| Preminimum | | .61** | | .57*** |
| Postminimum | | .20 | | .24 |

NOTE: Low-wage industries include tobacco, cigars, tobacco stemming, textiles, full-fashioned hosiery, apparel, men's and boys' nightshirts, trousers, sawmilling, millwork, containers, furniture, wood furniture, upholstered furniture, fertilizer, leather, leather tanning, footwear, and structural clay products.
** Significant at 5 percent level.
*** Significant at 2.5 percent level.
SOURCE: Kaun, "Economics of the Minimum Wage."

have worsened the long-term employment trends in the South relative to the non-South in low-wage manufacturing industries. It is precisely the trends and long-term adjustments that time series analysis of year-to-year fluctuations is ill adapted to reveal.

To sum up, the breakdown of data within the high-wage manufacturing division showed that some of its lowest-wage industries were as much affected by the minimum wage as was retailing. The negative effect on employment was clearer in more cases than on man-hours, suggesting that part-time employment was not as important in low-wage manufacturing industries as in retailing. The new minimum-wage measure isolated the minimum-wage effects more clearly than the conventional minimum-wage measure, and it showed a higher elasticity than was previously recognized. The immediate burden fell on low-wage industries everywhere, but the long-term effects on the South may have been greater.

# 6
# Summary

After more than three decades of experience with raises in federal minimum wages, the public is still little aware of their adverse effects on employment, especially for those disadvantaged workers most involved—the blacks, youth, and females. In spite of the inherent difficulties in isolating the effects of modest raises in minimums from the large independent increases in wages and employment economy-wide, numerous academic studies using statistical regression techniques have demonstrated the adverse nature of the employment effects. It is the magnitude of the effects that has remained controversial and seemingly small.

This study has pointed to a flaw in the methods used in these studies that tends to underestimate the effects. It is the conventional measure of the minimum wage itself that confuses the results. The measure—a coverage-weighted relative minimum wage—was developed by the BLS to take account of different coverage ratios by industry for two levels of minimum-wage rates as newly covered groups were phased in. The annually shifting elements in this measure—average wage, employment weights, and coverage ratios—introduce a feedback of the effects on the measure of what is supposed to be their cause. More serious, the mere division of the minimum wage by the average wage fails to take account of the distribution of wage levels among workers. It cannot show when the minimum is too low to be effective or how sharply the wage cost rises as more workers fall under successively higher minimum-wage rates.

A new measure—the relative minimum-wage impact—has been proposed in this study. This uses a concept long inherent in the annual Labor Department estimates of the percentage increase in payrolls required by each new minimum-wage rate. It is the first-order effect of raising below-minimum wages in a prior-period wage distribution before any adjustments by employers occur. It is proposed that a simple linear wage-distribution model can be used to extrapolate data between the years of Labor Department estimates to provide a continuous overall measure of the relative minimum-wage impact. Or, better, an industry-weighted form of the measure can be obtained from the 1970 wage-distribution data published by the Labor Department. This form also enables the relative minimum-wage impact to be computed for individual industries where annual wage data are available.

The empirical part of this study has tested the new measure in comparison with the conventional measure. For comparison, the conventional measure was slightly adjusted to eliminate the feedback characteristics of its weights. Both measures were applied in a series of industry time series regressions over the 1947–1979 period, and it was shown that the new measure provided more statistically significant estimates of the minimum-wage effects on employment. With its strong upward trend bias, the conventional measure sometimes failed even to show the expected sign.

The use of industry data reported by employing establishments in these empirical tests also permitted the use of man-hours as the measure of the resulting quantity of labor employed. Other studies of minimum-wage effects by type of worker have used data from the Bureau of the Census monthly household surveys, which report only number of workers employed or number of part-time workers. The results of this study showed that man-hours are a more sensitive measure of the amount of labor employed. Usually, the man-hour effects showed up more clearly in the regressions, although manufacturing industries tended to show little difference in significance between employment and man-hour effects.

A more complete overall picture of the employment effects by industry has been provided through the empirical testing of this study. The man-hour effects of a minimum were shown to be significantly adverse in all private nonfarm industries, though barely perceptible. For a breakdown into the eight major industry divisions, the new measure shows that only three divisions could be substantially affected, and of these only retail trade showed statistically significant positive effects of the minimum on the average wage. Accordingly, a significant adverse effect on man-hours could be shown only for retail trade. A third of the estimated all-industry man-hour losses occurred in this division, however.

Extending this breakdown approach within manufacturing, it was shown that only six of the twenty manufacturing industry groups were affected substantially throughout the three decades. Although significant positive minimum-wage effects on the average wage could be shown for only four of these, significant adverse effects on employment were shown for all six. Another key study cited showed that the adverse employment effects on low-wage industries as a group clearly occurred within both the North and the South, although the effects on all manufacturing did not show up any more clearly for the South than for the nation. Statistical regressions of year-by-year changes, however, are not useful to show the long-term effects on regions.

The most notable result of this empirical testing is the large size of the adverse employment effects. The economists' measure of demand elasticity—the ratio of the percentage change in employment divided by the percentage change in wage—usually has been estimated to be well below unity in other minimum-wage studies. This has led proponents of minimum-wage legislation to continue to view the adverse effects as small and more than offset by the benefits. In this study, however, the man-hour elasticity for below-minimum-wage workers was found to be —0.97 for all private nonfarm industries, —2.56 for retail trade, and —4.68 for leather products. The conventional minimum-wage measure consistently underestimated these elasticities.

These elasticity results have important implications for both legislators and research workers. While any minimum-wage rate may seem low in relation to an overall average wage, higher minimums involve a very rapid escalation in effects (as table 20, in the appendix, illustrates). National aggregates, therefore, are misleading; for a uniform minimum wage places discriminatory burdens on certain industries—the very industries upon which unskilled and disadvantaged workers most depend for jobs and income.

Uniform elasticity estimates also should not be expected as some sort of test of the validity of empirical research, for the elasticity may vary with the severity of the impact. The elasticity measure itself should also be constructed with caution. Some estimate of the proportion of workers whose wages are below the minimum and of their average wage is required to compare the imposed percentage wage increase and the percentage disemployment effect.

# Appendix

TABLE 13

MINIMUM-WAGE RATES UNDER THE FAIR LABOR STANDARDS ACT,
1938–1981
(in dollars)

| Year of Law and Amend-ments | Effective Dates for Rates | Minimum-Wage Rates by Coverage Status | | | | |
|---|---|---|---|---|---|---|
| | | Covered pre-1961 | Covered in 1961[a] | Covered in 1967[b] | Covered in 1974[c] | Farm covered |
| 1938 | October 1, 1938 | 0.25 | | | | |
| | October 1, 1939 | 0.30 | | | | |
| | 1940 | | | | | |
| | 1941 | | | | | |
| | 1942 | | | | | |
| | 1943 | | | | | |
| | 1944 | | | | | |
| | October 1, 1945 | 0.40 | | | | |
| | 1946 | | | | | |
| | 1947 | | | | | |
| | 1948 | | | | | |
| | 1949 | | | | | |
| 1949 | January 25, 1950 | 0.75 | | | | |
| | 1951 | | | | | |
| | 1952 | | | | | |
| | 1953 | | | | | |
| | 1954 | | | | | |
| | 1955 | | | | | |

*(Table continues)*

TABLE 13 (continued)

| Year of Law and Amendments | Effective Dates for Rates | Minimum-Wage Rates by Coverage Status | | | | |
|---|---|---|---|---|---|---|
| | | Covered pre-1961 | Covered in 1961[a] | Covered in 1967[b] | Covered in 1974[c] | Farm covered |
| 1956 | March 1, 1956 | 1.00 | | | | |
| | 1957 | | | | | |
| | 1958 | | | | | |
| | 1959 | | | | | |
| | 1960 | | | | | |
| 1961 | September 1, 1961 | 1.15 | 1.00 | | | |
| | 1962 | | | | | |
| | September 1, 1963 | 1.25 | | | | |
| | September 1, 1964 | | 1.15 | | | |
| | September 1, 1965 | | 1.25 | | | |
| | 1966 | | | | | |
| 1966 | February 1, 1967 | 1.40 | 1.40 | 1.00 | | 1.00 |
| | February 1, 1968 | 1.60 | 1.60 | 1.15 | | 1.15 |
| | February 1, 1969 | | | 1.30 | | 1.30 |
| | February 1, 1970 | | | 1.45 | | |
| | February 1, 1971 | | | 1.60 | | |
| | 1972 | | | | | |
| | 1973 | | | | | |
| 1974 | May 1, 1974 | 2.00 | 2.00 | 1.90 | 1.90 | 1.60 |
| | January 1, 1975 | 2.10 | 2.10 | 2.00 | 2.00 | 1.80 |
| | January 1, 1976 | 2.30 | 2.30 | 2.20 | 2.20 | 2.00 |
| | January 1, 1977 | | | 2.30 | 2.30 | 2.20 |
| 1977 | January 1, 1978 | 2.65 | 2.65 | 2.65 | 2.65 | 2.65 |
| | January 1, 1979 | 2.90 | 2.90 | 2.90 | 2.90 | 2.90 |
| | January 1, 1980 | 3.10 | 3.10 | 3.10 | 3.10 | 3.10 |
| | January 1, 1981 | 3.35 | 3.35 | 3.35 | 3.35 | 3.35 |

[a] Counted as newly covered in 1961, but included in basic after 1966.
[b] Counted as newly covered after 1966.
[c] Excluded from basic and new data series.
SOURCE: Furnished by U.S. Department of Labor.

# TABLE 14
## Some Minimum-Wage Measures, 1947–1979

| Year | Basic Minimum-Wage Rate[a] (dollars) | Average Hourly Earnings[b] (dollars) | Relative Basic Minimum Wage[a] (ratio) | Price Index (GDP Deflator)[b] (1972=1.000) | Real Basic Minimum Wage[a] (dollars) | Minimum-Wage Potential Index (1947–79 Av.=1.000) |
|------|------|------|------|------|------|------|
| 1947 | 0.40 | 1.131 | 0.354 | 0.507 | 0.789 | 0.442 |
| 1948 | 0.40 | 1.225 | 0.327 | 0.549 | 0.729 | 0.369 |
| 1949 | 0.40 | 1.275 | 0.314 | 0.554 | 0.722 | 0.342 |
| 1950 | 0.72 | 1.335 | 0.539 | 0.564 | 1.276 | 0.992 |
| 1951 | 0.75 | 1.45 | 0.517 | 0.600 | 1.250 | 0.914 |
| 1952 | 0.75 | 1.52 | 0.493 | 0.613 | 1.223 | 0.822 |
| 1953 | 0.75 | 1.61 | 0.466 | 0.627 | 1.196 | 0.736 |
| 1954 | 0.75 | 1.65 | 0.455 | 0.636 | 1.179 | 0.696 |
| 1955 | 0.75 | 1.71 | 0.439 | 0.649 | 1.156 | 0.651 |
| 1956 | 0.96 | 1.80 | 0.533 | 0.669 | 1.435 | 0.951 |
| 1957 | 1.00 | 1.89 | 0.529 | 0.691 | 1.447 | 0.938 |
| 1958 | 1.00 | 1.95 | 0.513 | 0.702 | 1.425 | 0.876 |
| 1959 | 1.00 | 2.02 | 0.495 | 0.718 | 1.393 | 0.819 |
| 1960 | 1.00 | 2.09 | 0.478 | 0.729 | 1.372 | 0.769 |
| 1961 | 1.05 | 2.14 | 0.491 | 0.733 | 1.432 | 0.848 |
| 1962 | 1.15 | 2.22 | 0.518 | 0.740 | 1.554 | 1.067 |
| 1963 | 1.18 | 2.28 | 0.518 | 0.748 | 1.578 | 1.067 |
| 1964 | 1.25 | 2.36 | 0.530 | 0.759 | 1.647 | 1.144 |
| 1965 | 1.25 | 2.46 | 0.508 | 0.768 | 1.628 | 1.085 |
| 1966 | 1.25 | 2.56 | 0.488 | 0.790 | 1.582 | 1.011 |
| 1967 | 1.39 | 2.68 | 0.519 | 0.816 | 1.703 | 1.352 |
| 1968 | 1.58 | 2.85 | 0.554 | 0.847 | 1.865 | 1.519 |
| 1969 | 1.60 | 3.04 | 0.526 | 0.885 | 1.808 | 1.481 |
| 1970 | 1.60 | 3.23 | 0.495 | 0.927 | 1.726 | 1.331 |
| 1971 | 1.60 | 3.45 | 0.464 | 0.970 | 1.649 | 1.168 |

*(Table continues)*

## TABLE 14 (continued)

| Year | Basic Minimum-Wage Rate[a] (dollars) | Average Hourly Earnings[b] (dollars) | Relative Basic Minimum Wage[a] (ratio) | Price Index (GDP Deflator)[b] (1972 = 1.000) | Real Basic Minimum Wage[a] (dollars) | Minimum-Wage Potential Index (1947–79 Av. = 1.000) |
|---|---|---|---|---|---|---|
| 1972 | 1.60 | 3.70 | 0.432 | 1.000 | 1.600 | 1.038 |
| 1973 | 1.60 | 3.94 | 0.406 | 1.047 | 1.528 | 0.907 |
| 1974 | 2.10 | 4.24 | 0.495 | 1.147 | 1.831 | 1.385 |
| 1975 | 2.30 | 4.54 | 0.507 | 1.264 | 1.820 | 1.403 |
| 1976 | 2.30 | 4.86 | 0.473 | 1.332 | 1.727 | 1.208 |
| 1977 | 2.30 | 5.25 | 0.438 | 1.410 | 1.631 | 1.040 |
| 1978 | 2.65 | 5.69 | 0.466 | 1.504 | 1.762 | 1.173 |
| 1979 | 2.90 | 6.16 | 0.471 | 1.632 | 1.777 | 1.216 |

[a] Annual averaged when increases occur in months other than January.
[b] Private nonfarm sector of the economy.
SOURCES: U.S. Department of Labor, Bureau of Labor Statistics, *Employment and Earnings, United States, 1909–78*, bulletin 1312-11, and monthly issues of *Employment and Earnings*.

## TABLE 15

COVERAGE RATIOS USED FOR OVERALL RELATIVE MINIMUM-WAGE IMPACT, 1950–1978

| Effective Date of Amendment Period | Employment-Weighted Coverage Ratio | | |
|---|---|---|---|
| | Basic covered | Newly covered | Total covered |
| January 1950 | .608 | — | .608 |
| March 1956 | .608 | — | .608 |
| September 1961 | .599 | .091 | .690 |
| February 1967 | .695 | .134 | .829 |
| May 1974 | .684 | .152 | .836 |
| January 1978 | .664 | .197 | .861 |

SOURCE: Based on summary tabulations by major industry division supplied by the Employment Standards Administration.

TABLE 16: ANALYSIS OF WEIGHTS IN THE BLS MINIMUM-WAGE MEASURE, 1950–1978

| Year | Item | Mining | Construction | Manufacturing | Transportation | Wholesale Trade | Retail Trade | Finance | Services |
|---|---|---|---|---|---|---|---|---|---|
| 1950 | W/W̄ | 1.327 | 1.316 | 1.079 | 1.139 | 1.070 | 0.734 | 1.004 | 0.794 |
| | Cov. | 0.99 | 0.44 | 0.95 | 0.88 | 0.69 | 0.03 | 0.74 | 0.19 |
| | Empl. | 0.023 | 0.060 | 0.389 | 0.103 | 0.067 | 0.173 | 0.048 | 0.137 |
| 1956 | W/W̄ | 1.289 | 1.427 | 1.083 | 1.156 | 1.078 | 0.722 | 0.989 | 0.794 |
| | Cov. | 0.99 | 0.44 | 0.95 | 0.88 | 0.69 | 0.03 | 0.74 | 0.19 |
| | Empl. | 0.018 | 0.067 | 0.383 | 0.094 | 0.067 | 0.174 | 0.053 | 0.144 |
| 1961 | W/W̄ | 1.234 | 1.495 | 1.084 | 1.210 | 1.079 | 0.729 | 0.977 | 0.818 |
| | Cov. | 0.99 | 0.80 | 0.96 | 0.95 | 0.69 | 0.33 | 0.74 | 0.22 |
| | Empl. | 0.015 | 0.163 | 0.359 | 0.086 | 0.069 | 0.181 | 0.059 | 0.168 |
| 1967 | W/W̄ | 1.190 | 1.533 | 1.056 | 1.209 | 1.078 | 0.750 | 0.963 | 0.854 |
| | Cov. | 0.99 | 0.99 | 0.97 | 0.97 | 0.72 | 0.486 | 0.74 | 0.631 |
| | Empl. | 0.011 | 0.060 | 0.357 | 0.078 | 0.068 | 0.182 | 0.059 | 0.185 |

(Table continues)

## TABLE 16 (continued)

| Year | Item | Mining | Construc-tion | Manu-facturing | Trans-portation | Wholesale Trade | Retail Trade | Finance | Services |
|------|------|--------|---------------|----------------|-----------------|-----------------|--------------|---------|----------|
| 1974 | $W/\overline{W}$ | 1.234 | 1.600 | 1.045 | 1.287 | 1.064 | 0.732 | 0.905 | 0.890 |
|      | Cov. | 0.993 | 0.995 | 0.974 | 0.982 | 0.800 | 0.637 | 0.762 | 0.718 |
|      | Empl. | 0.011 | 0.063 | 0.312 | 0.074 | 0.069 | 0.196 | 0.065 | 0.210 |
| 1978 | $W/\overline{W}$ | 1.348 | 1.520 | 1.084 | 1.330 | 1.033 | 0.736 | 0.861 | 0.877 |
|      | Cov. | 0.995 | 0.995 | 0.972 | 0.992 | 0.798 | 0.797 | 0.759 | 0.763 |
|      | Empl. | 0.012 | 0.060 | 0.289 | 0.069 | 0.070 | 0.206 | 0.067 | 0.227 |
| 1978 − 1950 | $W/\overline{W}$ | +.02 | +.20 | +.01 | +.19 | −.04 | .00 | −.14 | +.08 |
|      | Cov. | +.01 | +.56 | +.02 | +.11 | +.11 | +.77 | +.02 | +.57 |
|      | Empl. | −.01 | .00 | −.10 | −.03 | .00 | +.03 | +.02 | +.09 |

NOTE: Symbols: $W/\overline{W}$ = industry wage divided by all-industry average wage; Cov. = coverage ratio; Empl. = industry employment divided by all-industry employment.
SOURCE: Worksheets supplied by the Bureau of Labor Statistics.

## TABLE 17
### PAYROLL INCREASES ESTIMATED BY LABOR DEPARTMENT, 1950–1979

| Effective Date | Minimum-Wage Rate (dollars) | | Percentage of Workers below Minimum Wage | | Percent Payroll Increase Required | |
|---|---|---|---|---|---|---|
| | Basic | New | Basic | New | Basic | New |
| January 25, 1950 | 0.75 | | 6.21 | | 0.47 | |
| March 1, 1956 | 1.00 | | 8.34 | | 0.64 | |
| September 1, 1961 | 1.15 | 1.00 | 7.99 | 18.29 | 0.30 | 1.50 |
| September 1, 1963 | 1.25 | | 10.88 | | 0.33 | |
| September 1, 1964 | | 1.15 | | 15.69 | | 0.80 |
| September 1, 1965 | | 1.25 | | 22.50 | | 1.10 |
| February 1, 1967 | 1.40 | 1.00 | 11.50 | 10.31 | 0.47 | 0.90 |
| February 1, 1968 | 1.60 | 1.15 | 18.03 | 18.30 | 1.08 | 0.90 |
| February 1, 1969 | | 1.30 | | 20.17 | | 1.14 |
| February 1, 1970 | | 1.45 | | 19.68 | | 1.00 |
| May 1, 1974 | 2.00 | 1.90 | 3.72 | 14.14 | 0.17 | 0.92 |
| January 1, 1975 | 2.10 | 2.00 | 3.96 | 15.06 | 0.08 | 0.70 |
| January 1, 1976 | 2.30 | 2.20 | 3.36 | 13.03 | 0.13 | 0.59 |
| January 1, 1977 | | 2.30 | | 14.25 | | 0.45 |
| January 1, 1978 | 2.65 | 2.65 | 3.67 | 19.17 | 0.13 | 1.02 |
| January 1, 1979 | 2.90 | 2.90 | 3.86 | 21.02 | 0.13 | 0.83 |

NOTES: The data have been adjusted to remove government and farm workers. The payroll increase has been constructed for 1950.

SOURCES: U.S. Department of Labor, Employment Standards Administration, *Minimum Wage and Maximum Hours Standards under the Fair Labor Standards Act* (various years) and unpublished summary tables.

TABLE 18

## CUMULATIVE WAGE DISTRIBUTION BY COVERAGE STATUS, APRIL 1970

| Wage Rate (dollars) | Total | | Covered before 1967 | | Brought under, 1967 | | Largely Uncovered | |
|---|---|---|---|---|---|---|---|---|
| | % of wage | Cum. % of workers | % of wage | Cum. % of workers | % of wage | Cum. % of workers | % of wage | Cum. % of workers |
| 1.00 | | | | | | | 48.1 | 3.2 |
| 1.05 | | | | | | | 50.5 | 7.7 |
| 1.10 | | | | | | | 52.9 | 8.1 |
| 1.15 | | | | | | | 55.3 | 9.2 |
| 1.20 | | | | | | | 57.7 | 10.2 |
| 1.25 | | | | | | | 60.1 | 10.8 |
| 1.30 | | | | | | | 62.5 | 16.2 |
| 1.35 | | | | | | | 64.9 | 17.2 |
| 1.40 | | | | | | | 67.3 | 19.7 |
| 1.45 | 49.7 | 3.9 | | | 64.2 | 8.3 | 69.7 | 21.3 |
| 1.50 | 51.4 | 5.1 | | | 66.4 | 14.8 | 72.1 | 23.2 |
| 1.55 | 53.1 | 6.4 | | | 68.6 | 18.2 | 74.5 | 29.6 |
| 1.60 | 54.8 | 6.8 | 50.3 | 0.6 | 70.8 | 19.6 | 76.9 | 30.4 |
| 1.65 | 56.5 | 10.8 | 51.9 | 3.5 | 73.0 | 26.5 | 79.3 | 37.6 |
| 1.70 | 58.2 | 12.5 | 53.5 | 4.5 | 75.2 | 29.5 | 81.7 | 42.3 |
| 1.75 | 59.9 | 14.5 | 55.0 | 6.2 | 77.4 | 32.6 | 84.1 | 44.4 |
| 1.80 | 61.6 | 17.3 | 56.6 | 8.2 | 79.6 | 37.8 | 86.5 | 49.8 |
| 1.85 | 63.4 | 19.2 | 58.2 | 9.8 | 81.9 | 41.2 | 88.9 | 51.5 |
| 1.90 | 65.1 | 21.2 | 59.7 | 11.7 | 84.8 | 44.0 | 91.3 | 54.1 |
| 1.95 | 66.8 | 23.0 | 61.3 | 13.2 | 86.3 | 46.7 | 93.8 | 55.5 |
| 2.00 | 68.5 | 24.3 | 62.9 | 14.6 | 88.5 | 48.7 | 96.1 | 56.2 |
| 2.10 | 71.9 | 30.2 | 66.0 | 19.4 | 92.9 | 56.9 | 101.0 | 65.9 |
| 2.20 | 75.3 | 33.7 | 69.2 | 23.0 | 97.3 | 60.8 | 105.8 | 68.4 |
| 2.30 | 78.8 | 37.7 | 72.3 | 27.0 | 101.8 | 64.9 | 110.6 | 72.2 |
| 2.40 | 82.2 | 40.7 | 75.5 | 30.2 | 106.2 | 68.3 | 115.4 | 73.8 |
| 2.50 | 85.6 | 43.4 | 78.6 | 33.1 | 110.6 | 70.7 | 120.2 | 75.4 |
| Average hourly earnings (dollars) | 2.92 | | 3.18 | | 2.26 | | 2.08 | |
| Workers (millions) | 46.1 | | 34.1 | | 6.7 | | 5.3 | |

SOURCE: U.S. Department of Labor, Employment Standards Administration, *Wages and Hours of Work of Nonsupervisory Employees in All Private Nonfarm Industries by Coverage Status under the Fair Labor Standards Act* (1972).

# TABLE 19

## WAGE DISTRIBUTION PARAMETERS BY MAJOR INDUSTRY DIVISION, APRIL 1970

| Major Industry Division | Ratio of $w/\overline{W}$ with Zero Cumulative Workers ($R_0$) | Slope of Distribution ($b$) |
|---|---|---|
| Mining | n.a. | n.a. |
| Construction | 0.2977 | 0.593 |
| Manufacturing | 0.4951 | 1.086 |
| Transportation and public utilities | 0.7605 | 0.7605 |
| Wholesale trade | 0.5025 | 1.087 |
| Retail trade | | |
| Covered before 1967 | 0.6301 | 1.082 |
| Brought under coverage | 0.5372 | 1.882 |
| Finance | 0.5084 | 1.441 |
| Services | | |
| Covered before 1967 | 0.5370 | 1.097 |
| Brought under coverage | 0.4898 | 1.783 |

NOTE: Based on a linear regression for each industry of the cumulative percentage of workers and successively higher relative wage levels, expressed as a ratio to the industry mean ($R = w/\overline{W}$). The first column shows the horizontal axis intercept of the confidence limit two standard deviations above the regression line. It is the relative wage level ($R_0$) below which there are no workers. The second column shows the slope of the regression. The parameters for transportation may be substituted for mining. n.a. = not available.

SOURCE: Employment Standards Administration, *Wages and Hours of Work of Nonsupervisory Employees.*

## TABLE 20
### Comparison of Measures of Impact of Higher Minimum Wages

| Mini-mum-Wage Rate M ($) | Relative Mini-mum Wage M/W (ratio) | Mini-mum-Wage Potential M²/W (ratio) | Measures for Below-Minimum-Wage Workers | | | | Relative Mini-mum-Wage Impact (total) MI/W (%) |
|---|---|---|---|---|---|---|---|
| | | | w ($) | Δw ($) | Δw/w (ratio) | z (%) | |
| 1.30 | 0.4869 | 0.633 | n.a. | n.a. | 0 | 0 | 0 |
| 1.35 | 0.5056 | 0.683 | 1.336 | 0.014 | 0.0105 | 1.14 | 0.006 |
| 1.40 | 0.5243 | 0.734 | 1.361 | 0.039 | 0.0286 | 3.17 | 0.046 |
| 1.45 | 0.5431 | 0.788 | 1.386 | 0.064 | 0.0462 | 5.21 | 0.125 |
| 1.50 | 0.5618 | 0.843 | 1.411 | 0.089 | 0.0631 | 7.24 | 0.241 |
| 1.55 | 0.5805 | 0.900 | 1.436 | 0.114 | 0.0794 | 9.27 | 0.396 |
| 1.60 | 0.5993 | 0.959 | 1.461 | 0.139 | 0.0951 | 11.32 | 0.589 |
| 1.65 | 0.6180 | 1.020 | 1.486 | 0.164 | 0.1104 | 13.35 | 0.820 |
| Percent increases, from M = 1.50 to M = 1.65 | | | | | | | |
| | 10.0 | 21.0 | | | | 75.0 | 240.2 |

NOTES: This illustration is computed for manufacturing with an average wage (W) of $2.67 in 1967. The April 1970 wage distribution parameters were as follows: $R_0 = 49.51$; $b = 1.086$. The columns were computed as follows: $R_m = 100 \, M/W$; $R_w = [(R_m - R_0)/2] + R_0$; $w = R_w/100$; $\Delta w = (M - w)$; $z = (R_m - R_0)b$; $MI/W = \Delta wz/W$. n.a. = not available.
SOURCE: Author.

## TABLE 21
### Alternative Minimum-Wage Measures, All Private Nonfarm Industries, 1947–1979

| Year | Coverage-weighted Relative Minimum Wage | | Relative Minimum-Wage Impact | |
|---|---|---|---|---|
| | Conventional (MC/W*)[a] | Adjusted (MC/W)[b] | Overall (MI/W*)[c] | Industry-weighted (MI/W)[d] |
| 1947 | .203 | .223 | .000 | .000 |
| 1948 | .191 | .201 | .000 | .000 |
| 1949 | .180 | .185 | .000 | .000 |
| 1950 | .323 | .326 | .267 | .151 |
| 1951 | .301 | .317 | .172 | .033 |

## TABLE 21 (continued)

| Year | Coverage-weighted Relative Minimum Wage | | Relative Minimum-Wage Impact | |
|---|---|---|---|---|
| | Convential (MC/W\*)[a] | Adjusted (MC/W)[b] | Overall (MI/W\*)[c] | Industry-weighted (MI/W)[d] |
| 1952 | .284 | .299 | .070 | .025 |
| 1953 | .269 | .282 | .040 | .010 |
| 1954 | .258 | .268 | .015 | .004 |
| 1955 | .248 | .262 | .007 | .001 |
| 1956 | .307 | .306 | .327 | .077 |
| 1957 | .298 | .306 | .277 | .058 |
| 1958 | .283 | .293 | .191 | .031 |
| 1959 | .273 | .283 | .128 | .018 |
| 1960 | .262 | .275 | .083 | .009 |
| 1961 | .283 | .287 | .143 | .043 |
| 1962 | .328 | .343 | .284 | .097 |
| 1963 | .325 | .342 | .242 | .069 |
| 1964 | .334 | .350 | .240 | .103 |
| 1965 | .325 | .345 | .148 | .124 |
| 1966 | .315 | .291 | .093 | .117 |
| 1967 | .381 | .397 | .371 | .080 |
| 1968 | .412 | .434 | .785 | .269 |
| 1969 | .409 | .419 | .517 | .127 |
| 1970 | .400 | .400 | .256 | .053 |
| 1971 | .384 | .381 | .094 | .046 |
| 1972 | .363 | .358 | .022 | .016 |
| 1973 | .343 | .337 | .002 | .001 |
| 1974 | .369 | .378 | .145 | .039 |
| 1975 | .385 | .401 | .132 | .052 |
| 1976 | .401 | .410 | .176 | .085 |
| 1977 | .386 | .386 | .097 | .045 |
| 1978 | .416 | .438 | .271 | .217 |
| 1979 | .420 | .457 | .248 | .210 |

[a] Overall measure developed by the Bureau of Labor Statistics and extended by the Employment Standards Administration.

[b] Industry estimates (adjusted to be comparable with last column), employment weighted to an overall average.

[c] Using Labor Department annual reports on minimum wages to estimate wage impacts in increase years, interpolating for nonincrease years, holding coverage ratios fixed for amendment periods, dividing by prior-month average hourly earnings, holding ratios constant twelve months, and annual averaging.

[d] Industry estimates (as described in text) employment weighted to an overall average.

SOURCE: Author.

TABLE 22
COVERAGE-WEIGHTED RELATIVE MINIMUM WAGES BY MAJOR INDUSTRY DIVISION,
1947–1979
(ratio)

| Year | Mining | Construction | Manufacturing | Transportation | Wholesale Trade | Retail Trade | Finance | Services |
|------|--------|--------------|---------------|----------------|-----------------|--------------|---------|----------|
| 1947 | .289 | .120 | .339 | .329 | .237 | .015 | .277 | .088 |
| 1948 | .244 | .107 | .306 | .291 | .217 | .014 | .253 | .080 |
| 1949 | .227 | .099 | .281 | .254 | .204 | .013 | .241 | .079 |
| 1950 | .417 | .173 | .504 | .433 | .361 | .022 | .412 | .131 |
| 1951 | .408 | .169 | .488 | .425 | .349 | .022 | .399 | .131 |
| 1952 | .378 | .159 | .462 | .391 | .331 | .021 | .377 | .124 |
| 1953 | .351 | .149 | .434 | .369 | .315 | .020 | .359 | .117 |
| 1954 | .342 | .140 | .414 | .351 | .298 | .019 | .344 | .110 |
| 1955 | .344 | .136 | .406 | .339 | .290 | .018 | .331 | .107 |
| 1956 | .418 | .167 | .472 | .416 | .351 | .022 | .408 | .130 |
| 1957 | .415 | .167 | .471 | .415 | .351 | .022 | .412 | .130 |
| 1958 | .400 | .158 | .453 | .393 | .335 | .021 | .398 | .124 |
| 1959 | .387 | .153 | .437 | .373 | .323 | .021 | .287 | .120 |
| 1960 | .380 | .146 | .427 | .356 | .315 | .020 | .374 | .115 |

| Year | | | | | | | | |
|------|------|------|------|------|------|------|------|------|
| 1961 | .396 | .184 | .441 | .370 | .319 | .084 | .377 | .121 |
| 1962 | .431 | .369 | .488 | .412 | .342 | .211 | .402 | .140 |
| 1963 | .433 | .264 | .491 | .405 | .341 | .204 | .398 | .139 |
| 1964 | .448 | .268 | .505 | .413 | .349 | .207 | .408 | .142 |
| 1965 | .435 | .270 | .491 | .402 | .339 | .222 | .397 | .138 |
| 1966 | .417 | .266 | .476 | .391 | .327 | .224 | .383 | .131 |
| 1967 | .436 | .319 | .504 | .423 | .351 | .306 | .406 | .306 |
| 1968 | .476 | .342 | .544 | .463 | .382 | .331 | .445 | .349 |
| 1969 | .453 | .334 | .520 | .441 | .368 | .327 | .416 | .352 |
| 1970 | .423 | .308 | .491 | .417 | .345 | .318 | .394 | .350 |
| 1971 | .399 | .289 | .462 | .386 | .325 | .310 | .373 | .344 |
| 1972 | .368 | .269 | .436 | .351 | .304 | .293 | .352 | .323 |
| 1973 | .343 | .250 | .409 | .321 | .290 | .281 | .337 | .303 |
| 1974 | .363 | .282 | .445 | .347 | .335 | .364 | .380 | .346 |
| 1975 | .383 | .294 | .454 | .364 | .356 | .412 | .401 | .373 |
| 1976 | .369 | .302 | .465 | .365 | .365 | .428 | .414 | .380 |
| 1977 | .340 | .290 | .430 | .340 | .345 | .401 | .396 | .365 |
| 1978 | .389 | .318 | .455 | .357 | .378 | .527 | .450 | .407 |
| 1979 | .358 | .324 | .456 | .363 | .377 | .526 | .436 | .496 |

NOTE: This is the adjusted conventional measure as explained in chapter 2.
SOURCE: Based on worksheets supplied by the Bureau of Labor Statistics.

## TABLE 23

### Relative Minimum-Wage Impact by Major Industry Division, 1947–1979

(percent)

| Year | Mining | Construction | Manufacturing | Transportation | Wholesale Trade | Retail Trade | Finance | Services |
|---|---|---|---|---|---|---|---|---|
| 1947 | .000 | .000 | .000 | .000 | .000 | .000 | .000 | .000 |
| 1948 | .000 | .000 | .000 | .000 | .000 | .000 | .000 | .000 |
| 1949 | .000 | .000 | .000 | .000 | .000 | .000 | .000 | .000 |
| 1950 | .001 | .150 | .150 | .180 | .058 | .050 | .229 | .301 |
| 1951 | .000 | .100 | .025 | .084 | .005 | .032 | .057 | .228 |
| 1952 | .000 | .053 | .001 | .008 | .000 | .013 | .003 | .133 |
| 1953 | .000 | .021 | .000 | .000 | .000 | .004 | .000 | .061 |
| 1954 | .000 | .005 | .000 | .000 | .000 | .000 | .000 | .024 |
| 1955 | .000 | .002 | .000 | .000 | .000 | .000 | .000 | .009 |
| 1956 | .001 | .103 | .010 | .097 | .022 | .052 | .195 | .257 |
| 1957 | .000 | .085 | .002 | .051 | .005 | .040 | .126 | .230 |
| 1958 | .000 | .048 | .000 | .009 | .000 | .022 | .048 | .146 |
| 1959 | .000 | .031 | .000 | .001 | .000 | .012 | .013 | .090 |
| 1960 | .000 | .016 | .000 | .000 | .000 | .004 | .001 | .051 |
| 1961 | .000 | .036 | .006 | .001 | .051 | .113 | .031 | .074 |

| Year | | | | | | | | |
|------|------|------|------|------|------|------|------|------|
| 1962 | .001 | .085 | .012 | .003 | .103 | .283 | .070 | .146 |
| 1963 | .006 | .078 | .026 | .002 | .001 | .163 | .056 | .130 |
| 1964 | .014 | .098 | .055 | .003 | .001 | .228 | .101 | .173 |
| 1965 | .003 | .060 | .017 | .000 | .000 | .497 | .048 | .128 |
| 1966 | .000 | .031 | .001 | .000 | .000 | .565 | .007 | .069 |
| 1967 | .003 | .061 | .041 | .002 | .000 | .211 | .099 | .096 |
| 1968 | .086 | .122 | .242 | .084 | .052 | .519 | .433 | .238 |
| 1969 | .025 | .073 | .099 | .024 | .008 | .264 | .157 | .150 |
| 1970 | .002 | .013 | .012 | .001 | .000 | .138 | .033 | .112 |
| 1971 | .000 | .001 | .000 | .000 | .000 | .140 | .002 | .109 |
| 1972 | .000 | .000 | .000 | .000 | .000 | .068 | .000 | .020 |
| 1973 | .000 | .000 | .000 | .000 | .000 | .002 | .000 | .001 |
| 1974 | .000 | .001 | .000 | .000 | .000 | .173 | .027 | .017 |
| 1975 | .000 | .000 | .000 | .000 | .000 | .240 | .020 | .016 |
| 1976 | .000 | .002 | .000 | .000 | .000 | .372 | .066 | .037 |
| 1977 | .000 | .000 | .000 | .000 | .000 | .215 | .006 | .014 |
| 1978 | .000 | .015 | .000 | .000 | .000 | .782 | .184 | .160 |
| 1979 | .000 | .022 | .000 | .000 | .000 | .701 | .214 | .220 |

NOTE: This is the new measure developed from industry parameters as explained in chapter 3.

SOURCE: Author.

## TABLE 24

### Wage Effects in Major Industry Divisions, High-Wage Group, 1947–1979

| Dependent | Constant | Minimum-Wage Measure | Other Independent Variables | | | $R^2$ | Autoregressive (lag) | Correlation |
|---|---|---|---|---|---|---|---|---|
| **Construction** | | | | | | | | |
| $WAGE =$ | $-.4042$ | $- .0003\ MC/W$ (0.0) | $+ 1.481\ WH$ (25.6) | $+ 1.687\ D69$ (8.6) | $- .3669\ WHD$ (6.1) | .9986 | (2) | .088 |
| $WAGE =$ | $-.4108$ | $- .2653\ MI/W$ (0.8) | $+ 1.490\ WH$ (50.5) | $+ 1.654\ D69$ (11.4) | $- .3669\ WHD$ (9.5) | .9987 | (3) | $-.112$ |
| **Mining** | | | | | | | | |
| $WAGE =$ | $.3661$ | $+ .2632\ MC/W$ (1.0) | $+ .8884\ WH$ (29.5) | $- 1.623\ D69$ (13.0) | $+ .4410\ WHD$ (11.7) | .9989 | (3) | $-.056$ |
| $WAGE =$ | $.4209$ | $- .2182\ MI/W$ (0.3) | $+ .9095\ WH$ (38.0) | $- 1.551\ D69$ (13.3) | $+ .4150\ WHD$ (13.2) | .9988 | (3) | $-.088$ |

Transportation

$$WAGE = -.1616 - .1499\ MC/W + 1.142\ WH - .3178\ D69 + .0737\ WHD \qquad .9996 \quad (2) \quad -.044$$
$$\phantom{WAGE = -.1616 - .1499\ MC/W }(0.9)\phantom{MC/W} + (74.5)\phantom{WH} (4.2)\phantom{D69} (3.6)$$

WAGE = −.1616 − .1499 MC/W + 1.142 WH − .3178 D69 + .0737 WHD   .9996 (2) −.044
      (0.9)    (74.5)    (4.2)    (3.6)

WAGE = −.2021 − .0713 MI/W + 1.135 WH − .3426 D69 + .0828 WHD   .9996 (2) −.064
      (0.5)    (80.3)    (4.8)    (4.4)

Manufacturing

WAGE = .0880 + .0455 MC/W + .8956 WH − .2884 D69 + .0548 WHD   .9998 (2) .084
      (0.7)    (107.5)    (8.2)    (5.3)

WAGE = .0996 − .0200 MI/W + .8998 WH − .2763 D69 + .0504 WHD   .9998 (2) .098
      (0.3)    (125.6)    (8.4)    (5.5)

Wholesale

WAGE = .0228 − .0072 MC/W + .9312 WH + .3452 D69 − .1053 WHD   .9997 (3) −.055
      (0.1)    (94.0)    (8.4)    (9.2)

WAGE = .0210 + .0198 MI/W + .9314 WH + .3449 D69 − .1051 WHD   .9997 (3) −.054
      (0.1)    (113.9)    (8.6)    (9.8)

NOTES: Symbols for variables: $WAGE$ = average hourly earnings (\$); $MC/W$ = coverage-weighted relative minimum wage (ratio); $MI/W$ = relative minimum-wage impact (percent); $WH$ = average hourly earnings of high-wage group (\$); $D69$ = zero dummy becoming 1 after 1969; $WHD = WH \times D69$. In parentheses are $t$-values. None of the coefficients of the minimum-wage measures was significant.

SOURCES: Bureau of Labor Statistics, *Employment and Earnings, United States, 1909–78*, and monthly issues of *Employment and Earnings*.

93

TABLE 25:  WAGE EFFECTS IN MAJOR INDUSTRY DIVISIONS, POOLED LOW-WAGE GROUP, 1947–1979

| Dependent | Constant | | Minimum-Wage Measure | | Other Independent Variables | | | | |
|---|---|---|---|---|---|---|---|---|---|
| WAGE = | .0074 | + | .1983 $MC/W$ (5.5)*** | + | .6308 $WH1$ (73.6) | + | .2070 $D1$ (4.5) | − | .0566 $WHD1$ (4.5) |
| | | | | + | .8225 $WH2$ (83.2) | + | .6810 $D2$ (13.6) | − | .2027 $WHD2$ (15.2) |
| | | | | + | .7159 $WH3$ (70.7) | + | .0809 $D3$ (1.1) | + | .0054 $WHD3$ (0.3) |
| WAGE = | −.0028 | + | .0154 $MI/W$ (1.0) | + | .6535 $WH1$ (60.4) | + | .2183 $D1$ (3.9) | − | .0592 $WHD1$ (3.9) |
| | | | | + | .8556 $WH2$ (75.3) | + | .7847 $D2$ (11.5) | − | .2367 $WHD2$ (13.4) |
| | | | | + | .7350 $WH3$ (61.6) | + | .1022 $D3$ (1.3) | − | .0033 $WHD3$ (0.2) |

NOTES: Computed with the variance component technique, Parks method. The low-wage industry divisions are retail trade, finance, and services. Symbols for variables: $WAGE$ = average hourly earnings; $MC/W$ = coverage-weighted relative minimum wage (ratio); $MI/W$ = relative minimum-wage impact (percent); $WH1$, $WH2$, $WH3$ = wage average of high-wage industries (related to industries in sequence); $D1$, $D2$, $D3$ = zero dummies becoming 1 after 1969 (related in sequence); $WHD1$, $WHD2$, $WHD3$ = $WH \times D$ (for corresponding numbers). In parentheses are $t$-values, with significance percentages indicated for minimum-wage measures only.
*** Significant at 1 percent level.

SOURCES: Bureau of Labor Statistics, *Employment and Earnings, United States, 1909–78*, and monthly issues of *Employment and Earnings*.

## TABLE 26

### EMPLOYMENT EFFECTS IN MAJOR INDUSTRY DIVISIONS, HIGH-WAGE-GROUP, 1947–1979

| Dependent | Constant | Minimum-Wage Measure | Other Independent Variables | $R^2$ | Auto-regressive (lag) | Correlation |
|---|---|---|---|---|---|---|

**Construction**

$$NEMP = 1.455 - 1.264\ MC/W + .0043\ RGDP - .1612\ PROD + 3.891\ D65 - .4477\ PRD$$
$$(1.5)^* \qquad (5.3) \qquad (1.6) \qquad (3.1) \qquad (3.2)$$
$R^2 = .8759 \quad$ (lag) (2) $\quad$ Correlation .164

$$NEMP = 1.759 + .3262\ MI/W + .0043\ RGDP - .2409\ PROD + 2.988\ D65 - .3464\ PRD$$
$$(0.7) \qquad (5.7) \qquad (2.6) \qquad (2.8) \qquad (2.9)$$
$R^2 = .8808 \quad$ (lag) (3) $\quad$ Correlation −.093

**Mining**

$$NEMP = 1.849 - .0919\ MC/W + .0008\ RGDP - .2237\ PROD - 1.442\ D65 + .1636\ PRD$$
$$(0.5) \qquad (2.7) \qquad (6.2) \qquad (3.4) \qquad (3.4)$$
$R^2 = .8605 \quad$ (lag) (3) $\quad$ Correlation −.027

$$NEMP = 1.830 - .1501\ MI/W + .0007\ RGDP - .2234\ PROD - 1.535\ D65 + .1742\ PRD$$
$$(0.3) \qquad (2.5) \qquad (6.1) \qquad (4.0) \qquad (4.1)$$
$R^2 = .8561 \quad$ (lag) (3) $\quad$ Correlation −.010

**Transportation**

$$NEMP = 4.852 + .3378\ MC/W + .0024\ RGDP - .3759\ PROD - 1.064\ D65 + .1408\ PRD$$
$$(0.8) \qquad (4.2) \qquad (5.4) \qquad (1.3) \qquad (1.6)$$
$R^2 = .8282 \quad$ (lag) (2) $\quad$ Correlation .041

(Table continues)

## TABLE 26 (continued)

| Dependent | Constant | Minimum-Wage Measure | Other Independent Variables | $R^2$ | Auto-regressive (lag) | Correlation |
|---|---|---|---|---|---|---|
| $NEMP =$ | $4.935 +$ | $.1363\ MI/W$ <br>(0.4) | $+\ .0025\ RGDP - .3741\ PROD - .8068\ D65 + .1121\ PRD$ <br>(4.3) (5.3) (1.1) (1.4) | $.8304$ | $(3)$ | $-.045$ |
| **Manufacturing** | | | | | | |
| $NEMP =$ | $15.63 +$ | $3.433\ MC/W$ <br>(1.6)* | $+\ .0112\ RGDP - 1.474\ PROD + 8.802\ D65 - .8235\ PRD$ <br>(3.2) (3.5) (1.9) (1.6) | $.7687$ | $(4)$ | $.051$ |
| $NEMP =$ | $16.39 +$ | $1.879\ MI/W$ <br>(1.0) | $+\ .0124\ RGDP - 1.461\ PROD + 11.17\ D65 - 1.115\ PRD$ <br>(3.5) (3.4) (2.7) (2.4) | $.7370$ | $(4)$ | $.000$ |
| **Wholesale** | | | | | | |
| $NEMP =$ | $2.215 +$ | $.2611\ MC/W$ <br>(1.0) | $+\ .0034\ RGDP - .2137\ PROD - .8997\ D65 + .1001\ PRD$ <br>(9.6) (5.3) (2.1) (2.1) | $.9931$ | $(1)$ | $.049$ |
| $NEMP =$ | $2.263 -$ | $.1793\ MI/W$ <br>(0.5) | $+\ .0034\ RGDP - .2155\ PROD - .7385\ D65 + .0809\ PRD$ <br>(10.2) (5.2) (1.8) (1.8) | $.9925$ | $(1)$ | $.078$ |

NOTES: Symbols for variables: $NEMP$ = number of nonsupervisory workers employed (millions); $MC/W$ = coverage-weighted relative minimum wage (ratio); $MI/W$ = relative minimum-wage impact (percent); $RGDP$ = real gross domestic product, private nonfarm business ($ billions); $PROD$ = productivity index, private nonfarm business; $D65$ = zero dummy becoming 1 after 1965; $PRD$ = $D65 \times PROD$. In parentheses are $t$-values, with significance percentages indicated for minimum-wage measures only.

* Significant at 10 percent level.

SOURCE: See table 12.

TABLE 27

MAN-HOUR EFFECTS IN MAJOR INDUSTRY DIVISIONS, HIGH-WAGE GROUP, 1947–1979

| Dependent | Constant | Minimum-Wage Measure | Other Independent Variables | $R^2$ | Autoregressive (lag) | Correlation |
|---|---|---|---|---|---|---|
| **Construction** | | | | | | |
| $MANH =$ | 61.97 <br> | $- 41.13 \ MC/W$ <br> (1.2) | $+ .1653 \ RGDP$ <br> (4.9) $\quad - 7.699 \ PROD$ <br> (1.8) $\quad + 155.3 \ D69$ <br> (3.0) $\quad - 17.72 \ PRD$ <br> (3.1) | .8482 | (2) | .153 |
| $MANH =$ | 71.57 <br> | $+ 12.30 \ MI/W$ <br> (0.6) | $+ .1626 \ RGDP$ <br> (5.1) $\quad - 10.01 \ PROD$ <br> (2.5) $\quad + 124.2 \ D69$ <br> (2.8) $\quad - 14.21 \ PRD$ <br> (2.9) | .8552 | (3) | −.091 |
| **Mining** | | | | | | |
| $MANH =$ | 71.57 <br> | $- .9514 \ MC/W$ <br> (0.1) | $+ .0398 \ RGDP$ <br> (3.0) $\quad - 9.440 \ PROD$ <br> (5.8) $\quad - 51.33 \ D69$ <br> (2.7) $\quad + 5.818 \ PRD$ <br> (2.8) | .8333 | (3) | −.046 |
| $MANH =$ | 71.17 <br> | $- 3.122 \ MI/W$ <br> (0.1) | $+ .0391 \ RGDP$ <br> (3.0) $\quad - 9.379 \ PROD$ <br> (5.8) $\quad - 52.35 \ D69$ <br> (3.2) $\quad + 5.936 \ PRD$ <br> (3.3) | .8288 | (3) | −.040 |
| **Transportation** | | | | | | |
| $MANH =$ | 192.6 <br> | $+ 27.57 \ MC/W$ <br> (1.3)* | $+ .1060 \ RGDP$ <br> (3.6) $\quad - 15.99 \ PROD$ <br> (4.5) $\quad - 19.46 \ D69$ <br> (0.5) $\quad + 3.017 \ PRD$ <br> (0.7) | .7195 | (2) | .020 |

(Table continues)

## TABLE 27 (continued)

| Dependent | Constant | Minimum-Wage Measure | Other Independent Variables | | | | | $R^2$ | Auto-regressive (lag) | Correlation |
|---|---|---|---|---|---|---|---|---|---|---|

$$MANH = 197.5 + 18.44\ MI/W + .1116\ RGDP - 15.69\ PROD + 4.718\ D69 + .2584\ PRD$$
$$(1.1) \quad\quad (3.7) \quad\quad\quad (4.4) \quad\quad\quad (0.0) \quad\quad (0.2)$$
$R^2 = .7098$, (2), .020

**Manufacturing**

$$MANH = 620.6 + 190.2\ MC/W + .4998\ RGDP - 65.08\ PROD + 433.8\ D69 - 41.73\ PRD$$
$$(1.8)^* \quad\quad (2.8) \quad\quad\quad (3.1) \quad\quad\quad (1.9) \quad\quad (1.6)$$
$R^2 = .6988$, (4), .087

$$MANH = 663.2 + 109.2\ MI/W + .5623\ RGDP - 64.17\ PROD + 562.0\ D69 - 57.43\ PRD$$
$$(1.2) \quad\quad (3.1) \quad\quad\quad (3.0) \quad\quad\quad (2.7) \quad\quad (2.5)$$
$R^2 = .6644$, (4), .024

**Wholesale**

$$MANH = 92.04 + 4.713\ MC/W + .1351\ RGDP - 8.620\ PROD + 2.867\ D69 - .3427\ PRD$$
$$(0.6) \quad\quad (12.5) \quad\quad\quad (6.9) \quad\quad\quad (0.2) \quad\quad (0.2)$$
$R^2 = .9955$, (1), −.050

$$MANH = 92.81 - 6.600\ MI/W + .1366\ RGDP - 8.617\ PROD + 5.799\ D69 - .6974\ PRD$$
$$(0.6) \quad\quad (13.4) \quad\quad\quad (6.9) \quad\quad\quad (0.5) \quad\quad (0.5)$$
$R^2 = .9954$, (1), −.036

NOTES: Symbols for variables: $MANH$ = man-hours per week (millions); $MC/W$ = coverage-weighted relative minimum wage (ratio); $MI/W$ = relative minimum-wage impact (percent); $RGDP$ = real gross domestic product, private nonfarm business ($ billions); $PROD$ = productivity index, private nonfarm business; $D69$ = zero dummy becoming 1 after 1964; $PRD = D69 \times PROD$. In parentheses are $t$-values, with significance percentages indicated for minimum-wage measures only.

\* Significant at 10 percent level.

SOURCE: See table 24.

TABLE 28: Employment Effects in Major Industry Divisions, Pooled Low-Wage Group, 1947–1979

| Dependent | Constant | Minimum-Wage Measure | Other Independent Variables | | | |
|---|---|---|---|---|---|---|
| NEMP = | 2.203 | − .3397 MC/W (1.1) | + .0073 RG1 (5.9) | + .1598 PR1 (1.5) | − 5.381 D1 (2.8) | + .5796 PRD1 (2.7) |
| | | | + .0050 RG2 (6.9) | − .3391 PR2 (1.5) | + .0287 D2 (0.0) | + .0026 PRD2 (0.0) |
| | | | + .0149 RG3 (10.9) | − .5596 PR3 (4.8) | + 5.210 D3 (2.3) | + .5925 PRD3 (2.4) |
| NEMP = | 2.142 | − .1410 MI/W (1.6)* | + .0075 RG1 (6.4) | + .1497 PR1 (1.5) | − 4.510 D1 (2.3) | + .4804 PRD1 (2.2) |
| | | | + .0049 RG2 (7.4) | − .0402 PR2 (6.0) | − .2123 D2 (0.2) | + .0302 PRD2 (0.2) |
| | | | + .0149 RG3 (10.7) | − .0552 PR3 (4.8) | − 4.792 D3 (2.1) | + .5414 PRD3 (2.1) |

NOTES: Computed with the variance component technique, Parks method. The low-wage industry divisions are retail trade, finance, services. Symbols for variables: $NEMP$ = number of nonsupervisory workers employed (millions); $MC/W$ = coverage-weighted relative minimum wage (ratio); $MI/W$ = relative minimum-wage impact (percent); $RG1, RG2, RG3$ = real domestic product, private nonfarm business (related to industries in sequence) ($ billions); $PR1, PR2, PR3$ = productivity (related to industries in sequence); $D1, D2, D3$ = zero dummy becoming 1 after 1965 (related in sequence); $PRD1, PRD2, PRD3 = D \times PR$ (for corresponding numbers). In parentheses are $t$-values, with significance percentages indicated for minimum-wage measures only.

* Significant at 10 percent level.

SOURCES: Bureau of Labor Statistics, Employment and Earnings, United States, 1909-78, and monthly issues of Employment and Earnings.

TABLE 29: MAN-HOUR EFFECTS IN MAJOR INDUSTRY DIVISIONS, POOLED LOW-WAGE GROUP, 1947–1979

| Dependent | Constant | Minimum-Wage Measure | Other Independent Variables | | | | |
|---|---|---|---|---|---|---|---|
| MANH = | 94.07 | − 14.00 MC/W | + .1156 RG1 | + 17.28 PR1 | − 48.28 D1 | + 4.177 PRD1 | |
| | | (1.6)* | (2.8) | (5.1) | (0.7) | (0.5) | |
| | | | − .1907 RG2 | + 16.87 PR2 | + 1.692 D2 | + .2121 PRD2 | |
| | | | (7.1) | (6.9) | (0.0) | (0.0) | |
| | | | − .4507 RG3 | − 14.63 PR3 | − 76.16 D3 | + 9.032 PRD3 | |
| | | | (10.6) | (4.2) | (1.1) | (1.2) | |
| MANH = | 93.41 | − 5.947 MI/W | + .1222 RG1 | + 16.74 PR1 | − 20.59 D1 | + 1.046 PRD1 | |
| | | (2.4)*** | (3.1) | (5.1) | (0.3) | (0.1) | |
| | | | − .1850 RG2 | − 17.00 PR2 | − 16.49 D2 | + 2.277 PRD2 | |
| | | | (7.0) | (7.2) | (0.4) | (0.5) | |
| | | | − .4454 RG3 | − 14.27 PR3 | − 66.38 D3 | + 7.834 PRD3 | |
| | | | (10.5) | (4.1) | (0.9) | (1.0) | |

NOTES: Computed with the variance component technique, Parks method. The low-wage industry divisions are retail trade, finance, and services. Symbols for variables: $MANH$ = man-hours per week (millions); $MC/W$ = coverage-weighted relative minimum wage (ratio); $MI/W$ = relative minimum-wage impact (percent); $RG1$, $RG2$, $RG3$ = real domestic product, private nonfarm business (related to industries in sequence) ($ billions); $PR1$, $PR2$, $PR3$ = productivity index, private nonfarm business (in sequence); $D1$, $D2$, $D3$ = zero dummy becoming 1 after 1965 (in sequence); $PRD = D \times PR$ (for corresponding numbers). In parentheses are $t$-values, with significance percentages indicated for minimum-wage measures only.

\* Significant at 10 percent level.   \*\*\* Significant at 1 percent level.

SOURCES: Bureau of Labor Statistics, *Employment and Earnings, United States, 1909–78*, and monthly issues of *Employment and Earnings*.

## TABLE 30

### Wage Effects in Marginal Manufacturing Industries, 1947–1979

| Dependent | Constant | Minimum-Wage Measure | Other Independent Variables | | | $R^2$ | Auto-regressive (lag) | Correlation |
|---|---|---|---|---|---|---|---|---|

**Food**

$$WAGE = -.1338 - \underset{(0.7)}{.1565\ MC/W} + \underset{(34.7)}{.9367\ WH} + \underset{(0.4)}{.0426\ D69} - \underset{(0.5)}{.0164\ WD}$$

$R^2 = .9983$   (1)   $-.002$

$$WAGE = -.1915 - \underset{(0.9)}{.0480\ MI/W} + \underset{(40.7)}{.9304\ WH} - \underset{(0.2)}{.0267\ D69} - \underset{(0.4)}{.0107\ WD}$$

$R^2 = .9983$   (1)   $-.003$

**Tobacco**

$$WAGE = -.1853 - \underset{(1.2)}{.1985\ MC/W} + \underset{(34.9)}{.8413\ WH} - \underset{(8.9)}{.9298\ D69} + \underset{(9.3)}{.2898\ WD}$$

$R^2 = .9988$   (3)   $-.005$

$$WAGE = -.2695 - \underset{(0.4)}{.0055\ MI/W} + \underset{(34.0)}{.8277\ WH} - \underset{(8.5)}{.9654\ D69} + \underset{(9.8)}{.3074\ WD}$$

$R^2 = .9985$   (4)   $.006$

NOTES: Symbols for variables: $WAGE$ = average hourly earnings (\$); $MC/W$ = relative minimum-wage impact (percent); $WH$ = average hourly earnings of high-wage group, durables or nondurables manufacturing (\$); $D69$ = zero dummy becoming 1 after 1969; $WD = D69 \times WH$. In parentheses are $t$-values. None of the coefficients of the minimum-wage measures was significant.

SOURCES: Bureau of Labor Statistics, *Employment and Earnings, United States, 1909–78*, and monthly issues of *Employment and Earnings*.

## TABLE 31

### EMPLOYMENT AND MAN-HOUR EFFECTS IN MARGINAL MANUFACTURING INDUSTRIES, 1947–1979

| Dependent | Constant | Minimum-Wage Measure | | Other Independent Variables | | $R^2$ | Autoregressive | |
|---|---|---|---|---|---|---|---|---|
| | | | | | | | (lag) | Correlation |
| Food | | | | | | | | |
| NEMP = | .0990 | − | .0058 MC/W (1.1) | + | .0228 NH (5.2) − .0013 TIME (9.6) | .8103 | (4) | .217 |
| NEMP = | .0994 | − | .0008 MI/W (0.7) | + | .0211 NH (5.2) − .0012 TIME (9.3) | .7760 | (4) | .317 |
| MANH = | 49.02 | − | 2.041 MC/W (0.7) | + | .0133 MH (3.3) .5196 TIME (8.9) | .7786 | (4) | .255 |
| MANH = | 48.50 | − | .3760 MI/W (0.6) | + | .0131 MH (3.7) .5276 TIME (9.7) | .7377 | (4) | .373 |

## Tobacco

$$NEMP = 1.158 - .1629\ MC/W - .0015\ NH - .0160\ TIME \qquad .9888 \quad (4) \quad -.207$$
$$\phantom{NEMP = 1.158 - }(3.7)^{***} \qquad\qquad (0.0) \qquad\quad (13.0)$$

$$NEMP = 1.079 - .0205\ MI/W + .0015\ NH - .0163\ TIME \qquad .9892 \quad (4) \quad -.110$$
$$\phantom{NEMP = 1.079 - }(4.0)^{***} \qquad\qquad (0.0) \qquad\quad (13.5)$$

$$MANH = 44.72 - 4.424\ MC/W - .0018\ MH - .6081\ TIME \qquad .9884 \quad (4) \quad -.122$$
$$\phantom{MANH = 44.72 - }(2.6)^{***} \qquad\qquad (0.4) \qquad\quad (13.5)$$

$$MANH = 43.09 - .5362\ MI/W - .0024\ MH - .6080\ TIME \qquad .9886 \quad (4) \quad -.084$$
$$\phantom{MANH = 43.09 - }(2.5)^{***} \qquad\qquad (0.6) \qquad\quad (13.3)$$

NOTES: Symbols for variables: $NEMP$ = number of nonsupervisory workers employed (millions); $MANH$ = man-hours per week (millions); $MC/W$ = relative minimum wage (ratio); $MI/W$ = relative minimum-wage impact (percent); $NH$ = number employed in high-wage group, nondurables manufacturing (millions); $MH$ = man-hours per week in high-wage group, nondurables manufacturing (millions); $TIME$ = year minus 1946. In parentheses are $t$-values, with significance indicated for minimum-wage measures only.

*** Significant at 1 percent level.

SOURCES: Bureau of Labor Statistics, *Employment and Earnings, United States, 1909–78*, and monthly issues of *Employment and Earnings*.

103

## TABLE 32
### Employment Effects in Manufacturing Industries in Terms of Trends and Deviations, 1947–1974
#### (quarterly)

| Industry | Elasticities with Respect to a Minimum Wage | | |
| | For trend shares (1) | For deviation shares (2) | Differences (2) − (1) |
| --- | --- | --- | --- |
| Ordnance | 1.3709[b] | 5.4569 | 4.0860 |
| Lumber[a] | −0.0793 | −0.3527 | −0.2734 |
| Furniture[a] | −0.0041 | −0.8993 | −0.8952 |
| Stone-clay-glass | 0.0634[b] | −1.0632 | −1.0996 |
| Primary metals | 0.0831[c] | −0.6735 | 0.7566 |
| Fabricated metals | 0.1033[b] | −0.6115 | −0.7148 |
| Machinery | 0.0261 | −0.3061 | −0.3322 |
| Electrical equipment | 0.3121[b] | 0.7457[c] | 0.4336 |
| Transportation equipment | 0.3795[b] | 1.6290[c] | 1.2495 |
| Instruments | 0.1273 | −1.1402 | −1.2675 |
| Miscellaneous[a] | −0.0573 | −0.3748 | −0.3175 |
| Food | 0.0818[b] | 2.1208 | 2.0390 |
| Tobacco | 0.0030 | −1.3837 | −1.3867 |
| Textiles[a] | −0.2212 | −0.3408 | −0.1196 |
| Apparel[a] | 0.0782[b] | 1.7504[b] | 1.6722 |
| Paper | 0.1970 | 2.2104 | 2.0134 |
| Printing | 0.1246[b] | 2.7798[b] | 2.6552 |
| Chemicals | 0.1846 | 1.6560[b] | 1.4714 |
| Petroleum | 0.0411 | 1.4537 | 1.4126 |
| Rubber[a] | −0.1054 | −0.3754 | −0.2700 |
| Leather[a] | −0.1293 | −1.0152 | −0.8859 |

[a] Industries with a 1974 wage below $4.

[b] Indicates t-value greater than 3.

[c] Indicates t-value greater than 2.

Source: J. Wilson Mixon and Noel D. Uri, "The Effects of Minimum Wages on the Distribution of Changes in Aggregate Employment among Manufacturing Industries," *Review of Business and Economic Research* (Winter 1977–78), pp. 56–70.

## TABLE 33

### Effects on a Low-Wage Manufacturing Group, 1947–1966
(quarterly)

| Dependent | Minimum-Wage Measure | Other Independent Variables | $R^2$ | DW |
|---|---|---|---|---|
| $\ln W =$ | $-.0445 \ln (1-M/W_{-1})$ (10.8) | $+ .7595 \ln W_h$ (15.5) $\quad - .3082\,T$ (6.2) $\quad + .14\,T^2$ (7.5) | .999 | 2.03 |
| $\ln N =$ | $.0239 \ln (1-M/W_{-1})$ (3.8) $\quad + .3189 \ln N_{-1}$ (4.3) | $+ .4963 \ln N_h$ (7.3) $\quad + .0533\,T$ (4.0) $\quad - .02\,T^2$ (1.4) | .94 | 2.04 |
| $\ln M =$ | $.0401 \ln (1-M/W_{-1})$ (4.2) $\quad + .0078 \ln M_{-1}$ (0.1) | $+ .7946 \ln M_h$ (9.3) $\quad + .1126\,T$ (5.5) $\quad - .05\,T^2$ (2.7) | .92 | 2.72 |

Notes: The low-wage industries in the group (with standard industrial classification—SIC—codes) are: confectionery (207), tobacco (21), men's-boys' furnishings (232), girls'-children's outerwear (236), fertilizers—complete (2871), fertilizers—mixing (2972), and footwear (314). Symbols of variables: $W$ = wage; $N$ = number of nonsupervisory workers employed; $M$ = man-hours per week; $T$ = year minus 1946; $M/W_{-1}$ = relative minimum wage with prior-period wage (the subtraction from 1 in the minimum-wage measures is necessary for logarithms and reverses the sign of the coefficient that is predicted in theory); $h$ indicates high-wage industries; ln indicates logarithm. In parentheses are $t$-values; $t$-values exceeding 2.4 are significant at the 1 percent level. DW = Durbin-Watson statistic.

Source: Albert Zucker, "Minimum Wages and the Long-Run Elasticity of Demand for Low-Wage Labor," *Quarterly Journal of Economics* (May 1973), pp. 265–79.

TABLE 34

| Dependent | Constant | Minimum-Wage Measure | Other Independent Variables |
|---|---|---|---|

**Durables industries**

$$WAGE = .1467 + .0416\, MC/W + .7049\, WH1 - .4221\, D69 + .1478\, WD1$$
$$(0.8) \qquad\qquad (44.4) \qquad (4.8) \qquad\quad (6.3)$$

$$+ .6893\, WH2 + .3085\, D69 - .0736\, WD2$$
$$(44.3) \qquad\quad (3.8) \qquad\qquad (3.4)$$

$$+ .6946\, WH3 + .4113\, D69 - .0946\, WD3$$
$$(46.3) \qquad\quad (5.9) \qquad\qquad (4.8)$$

$$WAGE = .1662 + .0030\, MI/W + .7052\, WH1 - .4172\, D69 + .1471\, WD1$$
$$(0.3) \qquad\qquad (49.2) \qquad (5.1) \qquad\quad (6.9)$$

$$+ .6898\, WH2 + .3145\, D69 - .0747\, WD2$$
$$(49.2) \qquad\quad (4.3) \qquad\qquad (3.8)$$

$$+ .6949\, WH3 + .4161\, D69 - .0950\, WD3$$
$$(51.5) \qquad\quad (6.7) \qquad\qquad (5.5)$$

**Nondurables industries**

$$WAGE = .5012 - .1471\, MC/W + .4998\, WH1 - .3743\, D64 + .1595\, WD1$$
$$(1.4)^* \qquad\qquad (17.9) \qquad (4.2) \qquad\quad (5.0)$$

$$+ .5052\, WH2 - .0594\, D66 + .0474\, WD2$$
$$(18.8) \qquad\quad (0.7) \qquad\qquad (1.6)$$

$$+ .5213\, WH3 + .0036\, D69 + .0211\, WD3$$
$$(20.0) \qquad\quad (0.0) \qquad\qquad (0.6)$$

$$WAGE = .5064 + .0097\, MI/W + .4495\, WH1 - .5434\, D64 + .2193\, WD1$$
$$(1.1) \qquad\qquad (18.1) \qquad (6.1) \qquad\quad (7.1)$$

## TABLE 34 (continued)

| Depen-<br>dent | Con-<br>stant | Minimum-<br>Wage<br>Measure | Other Independent Variables |
|---|---|---|---|
| | | | $+ .4574\ WH2 - .1968\ D66 + .0968\ WD2$<br>(10.3)       (2.5)       (3.6) |
| | | | $+ .4768\ WH3 - .1380\ D69 + .0664\ WD3$<br>(20.5)       (1.1)       (1.9) |

NOTES: Computed with the variance component technique, Parks method. Durables industries: lumber, furniture, miscellaneous. Nondurables industries: textiles, apparel, leather. Symbols for variables: $WAGE$ = average hourly earnings (\$); $MC/W$ = relative minimum wage (ratio); $MI/W$ = relative minimum-wage impact (percent); $WH1$, $WH2$, $WH3$ = average hourly earnings for high-wage group, durables and nondurables manufacturing (related to industries in sequence); $D64$, $D66$, $D69$ = zero dummies becoming 1 after indicated year; $WD1$, $WD2$, $WD3$ = $D \times WH$ (for corresponding numbers). In parentheses are $t$-values, with significance percentage indicated for minimum-wage measures only.

* Significant at 10 percent level.

SOURCES: Bureau of Labor Statistics, *Employment and Earnings, United States, 1909-78*, and monthly issues of *Employment and Earnings*.

## TABLE 35

### EMPLOYMENT EFFECTS IN POOLED LOW-WAGE MANUFACTURING INDUSTRIES, 1947–1979

| Dependent | Constant | Minimum-Wage Measure | Other Independent Variables |
|---|---|---|---|

**Durables industries**

$$NEMP = .1943 - \underset{(2.7)^{***}}{.0561\ MC/W} + \underset{(12.7)}{.1107\ NH1} - \underset{(2.1)}{.3158\ D1} - \underset{(0.9)}{.0218\ ND1} + \underset{(2.5)}{.4347\ D2} - \underset{(3.2)}{.0881\ ND2}$$

$$+ \underset{(2.6)}{.0216\ NH2} + \underset{(0.5)}{.0408\ D3} - \underset{(0.5)}{.0067\ ND3} + \underset{(2.5)}{.1837\ D4} + \underset{(3.0)}{.0362\ ND4}$$

$$+ \underset{(4.0)}{.0332\ NH3} - \underset{(0.8)}{.0465\ D5} + \underset{(0.0)}{.0004\ ND5} + \underset{(1.7)}{.0718\ D6} - \underset{(1.8)}{.0120\ ND6}$$

$$NEMP = .2049 - \underset{(2.7)^{***}}{.0096\ MI/W} + \underset{(11.9)}{.1047\ NH1} - \underset{(2.5)}{.3775\ D1} + \underset{(1.3)}{.0317\ ND1} + \underset{(2.7)}{.4496\ D2} - \underset{(3.4)}{.0906\ ND2}$$

$$+ \underset{(1.8)}{.0153\ NH2} + \underset{(0.3)}{.0228\ D3} - \underset{(0.3)}{.0039\ ND3} + \underset{(2.9)}{.2085\ D4} + \underset{(3.6)}{.0041\ ND4}$$

$$+ \underset{(3.2)}{.0271\ NH3} - \underset{(1.4)}{.0884\ D5} + \underset{(0.6)}{.0072\ ND5} + \underset{(1.5)}{.0718\ D6} - \underset{(1.5)}{.0119\ ND6}$$

Nondurables industries

$$NEMP = .3156 - .0369 \, MC/W + .3668 \, NH1 + .9708 \, D1 - .5267 \, ND1 - .7972 \, D2 + .3027 \, ND2$$
$$(0.8) \quad\quad (5.2) \quad\quad (2.0) \quad\quad (2.3) \quad\quad (1.1) \quad\quad (1.0)$$

$$+ .4113 \, NH2 + .4332 \, D3 + .1979 \, ND3 + .0389 \, D4 - .0494 \, ND4$$
$$(6.1) \quad\quad (1.8) \quad\quad (1.7) \quad\quad (0.1) \quad\quad (0.4)$$

$$+ .0246 \, NH3 + .2769 \, D5 - .1412 \, ND5 + .2515 \, D6 + .0842 \, ND6$$
$$(0.4) \quad\quad (1.6) \quad\quad (1.6) \quad\quad (1.5) \quad\quad (1.2)$$

$$NEMP = .3972 - .0057 \, MI/W + .3162 \, NH1 + .8112 \, D1 - .4483 \, ND1 - .6758 \, D2 + .2499 \, ND2$$
$$(1.4)* \quad\quad (4.7) \quad\quad (1.7) \quad\quad (2.0) \quad\quad (0.9) \quad\quad (0.8)$$

$$+ .3600 \, NH2 + .2591 \, D3 + .1083 \, ND3 + .1851 \, D4 - .1160 \, ND4$$
$$(5.6) \quad\quad (1.2) \quad\quad (1.0) \quad\quad (0.6) \quad\quad (0.9)$$

$$- .0265 \, NH3 + .1184 \, D5 - .0607 \, ND5 + .1784 \, D6 + .0505 \, ND6$$
$$(0.4) \quad\quad (0.7) \quad\quad (0.7) \quad\quad (1.0) \quad\quad (0.7)$$

NOTES: Computed with the variance component technique, Parks method. Durables industries are lumber, furniture, and miscellaneous. Nondurables industries are textiles, apparel, and leather. Symbols for variables: $NEMP$ = number of nonsupervisory workers employed (millions); $MC/W$ = relative minimum wage (ratio); $MI/W$ = relative minimum-wage impact (percent); $NH1$, $NH2$, $NH3$ = number employed in high-wage group, durables or nondurables manufacturing (millions; related to industries in sequence); $D$ = zero dummy becoming 1 after certain year (1951 and 1961 for each durables industry and 1961 and 1969 for each nondurables industry); $ND = D \times NH$ (for corresponding numbers). In parentheses are $t$-values, with significance percentages indicated for minimum-wage measures only.

* Significant at 10 percent level.

*** Significant at 1 percent level.

SOURCES: Bureau of Labor Statistics, *Employment and Earnings, United States, 1909–78*, and monthly issues of *Employment and Earnings*.

## TABLE 36

### MAN-HOUR EFFECTS IN POOLED LOW-WAGE MANUFACTURING INDUSTRIES, 1947–1979

| Dependent | Constant | Minimum-Wage Measure | Other Independent Variables |
|---|---|---|---|

**Durables industries**

$$MANH = 7.974 - 1.747\ MC/W + 1.053\ MH1 - 9.251\ D1 + .0665\ MD1 + 14.87\ D2 - .7310\ MD2$$
$$(1.6)^* \qquad\quad (12.0) \qquad\quad (1.7) \qquad\quad (0.3) \qquad\quad (2.4) \qquad\quad (3.0)$$

$$+ .2054\ MH2 + .9439\ D3 - .0454\ MD3 + 6.500\ D4 + .3141\ MD4$$
$$(2.4) \qquad\quad (0.3) \qquad\quad (0.4) \qquad\quad (2.2) \qquad\quad (2.7)$$

$$+ .3127\ MH3 + 2.465\ D5 + .0205\ MD5 + 2.711\ D6 - .1225\ MD6$$
$$(3.7) \qquad\quad (1.0) \qquad\quad (0.2) \qquad\quad (1.5) \qquad\quad (1.7)$$

$$MANH = 8.148 - .3304\ MI/W + 1.016\ MH1 - 10.95\ D1 + .1301\ MD1 + 15.22\ D2 - .7444\ MD2$$
$$(1.9)^{**} \qquad\quad (12.0) \qquad\quad (2.1) \qquad\quad (0.6) \qquad\quad (2.5) \qquad\quad (3.2)$$

$$+ .1655\ MH2 + .4675\ D3 - .0289\ MD3 + 7.259\ D4 + .3467\ MD4$$
$$(2.0) \qquad\quad (0.2) \qquad\quad (0.2) \qquad\quad (2.6) \qquad\quad (3.2)$$

$$+ .2727\ MH3 + 3.552\ D5 + .0622\ MD5 + 2.667\ D6 - .1194\ MD6$$
$$(3.3) \qquad\quad (1.4) \qquad\quad (0.6) \qquad\quad (1.3) \qquad\quad (1.5)$$

Nondurables industries

$$MANH = 69.03 - 19.25\ MC/W - .0236\ MH1 - 41.31\ D1 + .0461\ MD1 + 6.812\ D2 - .0111\ MD2$$
$$(3.3)^{***} \quad (1.8) \quad (2.4) \quad (2.3) \quad (0.3) \quad (0.5)$$

$$- .0252\ MH2 - 35.46\ D3 + .0496\ MD3 - 2.854\ D4 - .0004\ MD4$$
$$(1.9) \quad (1.6) \quad (1.9) \quad (0.1) \quad (0.0)$$

$$+ .0881\ MH3 + 116.2\ D5 - .1494\ MD5 + 56.45\ D6 + .0336\ MD6$$
$$(6.5) \quad (2.7) \quad (3.1) \quad (0.9) \quad (0.5)$$

$$MANH = 67.88 - 2.013\ MI/W - .0338\ MH1 - 48.72\ D1 + .0571\ MD1 + 14.95\ D2 - .0216\ MD2$$
$$(3.7)^{***} \quad (2.9) \quad (3.0) \quad (3.1) \quad (0.7) \quad (0.9)$$

$$- .0353\ MH2 - 42.41\ D3 + .0599\ MD3 - 4.178\ D4 - .0004\ MD4$$
$$(3.0) \quad (2.0) \quad (2.5) \quad (0.1) \quad (0.0)$$

$$+ .0777\ MH3 + 100.9\ D5 - .1301\ MD5 + 52.45\ D6 + .0280\ MD6$$
$$(6.5) \quad (2.4) \quad (2.8) \quad (0.8) \quad (0.4)$$

NOTES: Computed with the variance component technique, Parks method. Durables are lumber, furniture, and miscellaneous. Nondurables are textiles, apparel, and leather. Symbols for variables: $MANH$ = man-hours per week (millions); $MC/W$ = relative minimum wage (ratio); $MI/W$ = relative minimum-wage impact (percent); $MH1$, $MH2$, $MH3$ = man-hours in high-wage group, durables or nondurables industries (related to industries in sequence) (millions); $D$ = zero dummy becoming 1 after certain year (1951 and 1961 for durables and 1961 and 1969 for nondurables); $MD = D \times MH$ (for corresponding numbers). In parentheses are $t$-values, with significance percentages indicated for minimum-wage measures only.

\* Significant at 10 percent level.

\*\* Significant at 5 percent level.

\*\*\* Significant at 1 percent level.

SOURCES: Bureau of Labor Statistics, *Employment and Earnings, United States, 1909–78*, and monthly issues of *Employment and Earnings*.

## TABLE 37

### MINIMUM-WAGE EFFECTS IN MANUFACTURING, BY WAGE LEVEL AND BY REGION, 1951–1973

| Dependent | Constant | Minimum-Wage Measure | Other Independent Variables | | | | | $R^2$ | DW |
|---|---|---|---|---|---|---|---|---|---|
| **North (all manufacturing)** | | | | | | | | | |
| $\ln W_n =$ | $1.26$ | $- .050\, M_n$ $(0.9)$ | $- .06\ \ln G$ $(0.6)$ | $- .010\, T$ $(1.0)$ | $+ .0017\, T^2$ $(5.7)$ | | | $.999$ | $1.68$ |
| $\ln E_n =$ | $-6.48$ | $+ .056\, M_n$ $(0.7)$ | $+ 1.51\ \ln G$ $(9.1)$ | $- .046\, T$ $(9.4)$ | $- .0003\, T^2$ $(2.5)$ | $+ .30 \ln E_{n-1}$ $(3.4)$ | | $.896$ | $2.07$ |
| $\ln MH_n =$ | $-6.79$ | $+ .024\, M_n$ $(0.3)$ | $+ 1.84\ \ln G$ $(11.9)$ | $- .056\, T$ $(12.0)$ | $- .0005\, T^2$ $(3.7)$ | $+ .14 \ln MH_{n-1}$ $(1.9)$ | | $.934$ | $2.14$ |
| **South (all manufacturing)** | | | | | | | | | |
| $\ln W_s =$ | $-.42$ | $- .078\, M_s$ $(4.0)^{***}$ | $- 1.21\ \ln W_n$ $(17.1)$ | $- .007\, T$ $(3.0)$ | $+ .0006\, T^2$ $(1.2)$ | | | $.999$ | $1.51$ |
| $\ln E_s =$ | $.14$ | $- .006\, M_s$ $(0.2)$ | $+ .67\ \ln E_n$ $(13.8)$ | $+ .009\, T$ $(5.3)$ | $+ .0005\, T^2$ $(8.3)$ | | | $.996$ | $1.75$ |
| $\ln MH_s =$ | $-.17$ | $+ .004\, M_s$ $(0.1)$ | $+ .71\ \ln MH_n$ $(14.6)$ | $+ .014\, T$ $(7.5)$ | $+ .0004\, T^2$ $(5.4)$ | | | $.996$ | $1.79$ |

High-wage (nationally)

$$\ln W_h = 1.44 - .047\, M_h - .07\, \ln G - .016\, T + .0018\, T^2 \qquad .998 \quad 1.64$$
$$\phantom{\ln W_h = 1.44} (0.8) \qquad (0.6) \qquad (1.3) \qquad (5.4)$$

$$\ln E_h = -7.03 + .032\, M_h + 1.49\, \ln G - .042\, T - .0003\, T^2 \qquad .947 \quad 2.18$$
$$\phantom{\ln E_h = -7.03} (0.4) \qquad (9.1) \qquad (9.0) \qquad (2.2)$$

$$\ln MH_h = -7.26 + .011\, M_h + 1.80\, \ln G - .050\, T - .0004\, T^2 + .35\, \ln E_{h-1} \qquad .961 \quad 2.16$$
$$\phantom{\ln MH_h = -7.26} (0.2) \qquad (12.3) \qquad (11.9) \qquad (3.5) \qquad (4.5)$$

Low-wage (nationally)

$$\ln W_l = -.06 - .079\, M_l + .570\, \ln W_n - .014\, T + .0010\, T^2 \qquad .999 \quad 1.40$$
$$\phantom{\ln W_l = -.06} (5.8)^{***} \quad (11.3) \qquad (6.9) \qquad (25.5)$$

$$\ln E_l = 1.70 + .056\, M_l + .57\, \ln E_n - .018\, T + .0005\, T^2 \qquad .894 \quad 1.90$$
$$\phantom{\ln E_l = 1.70} (1.4)^{*} \quad (7.1) \qquad (5.3) \qquad (3.8)$$

$$\ln MH_l = .88 + .059\, M_l + .66\, \ln MH_n - .013\, T + .0003\, T^2 + .20\, \ln MH_{h-1} \qquad .895 \quad 1.78$$
$$\phantom{\ln MH_l = .88} (1.5)^{*} \quad (8.9) \qquad (3.8) \qquad (2.5) \qquad (2.9)$$

NOTES: Low-wage industries include textiles, apparel, lumber, furniture, leather. High-wage industries include all other manufacturing. Symbols for variables: $M = (1 - M/W_{-1})$, 1 minus the relative minimum wage with a lagged wage deflator; $W$ = average hourly earnings (\$); $E$ = employed workers (thousands); $MH$ = man-hours per week (millions); $G$ = real gross national product; $T$ = year minus 1946. The ln indicates a log of the variable. In parentheses are $t$-values, with significance levels indicated for minimum-wage measure only. $DW$ = Durbin-Watson statistic. Note that the subtraction of the relative minimum wage reverses all expected signs on the coefficients.

* Significant at 10 percent level.

*** Significant at 1 percent level.

SOURCE: Joyce M. Nussbaum and Donald E. Wise, "The Impact of the Federal Minimum Wage on the Geographic Distribution of Employment," prepared by Mathtech, Inc., Princeton, New Jersey, for the U.S. Department of Labor, February 1977 (processed, National Technical Information Service, no. PB 266070).

A Note on the Book

The typeface used for the text of this book is
Palatino, designed by Hermann Zapf.
The type was set by
Hendricks-Miller Typographic Company, of Washington.
Thomson-Shore, Inc., of Dexter, Michigan, printed
and bound the book, using Warren's Olde Style paper.
The cover and format were designed by Pat Taylor,
and the figures were drawn by Hördur Karlsson.
The manuscript was edited by Joanne Ainsworth, and
by Gertrude Kaplan of the AEI Publications staff.

## Selected AEI Publications

## AEI Associates Program